10 Building Blocks
FOR A
Solid Family

THE **HOMEWORD** GUIDE TO **PARENTING**

JIM BURNS

Regal

From Gospel Light
Ventura, California, U.S.A.

Published by Regal
From Gospel Light
Ventura, California, U.S.A.
www.regalbooks.com
Printed in the U.S.A.

Originally published as *How to Be a Happy, Healthy Family* by W Publishing Group in
association with Yates and Yates, LLP, Literary Agents, Orange, CA, 2001.

First edition published in 2003.
Second edition published in 2010.

Library of Congress Cataloging-in-Publication Data
Burns, Jim, 1953–
[How to be a happy, healthy family]
The 10 building blocks for a solid family / Jim Burns.
p. cm.
Includes bibliographical references.
ISBN 0-8307-3302-7
1. Family—Religious life. 2. Parenting—Religious
aspects—Christianity. I. Title: Ten building blocks for a happy
family. II. Title.
BV4526.3.B87 2003
248.8'45—dc22
2003015362

1 2 3 4 5 6 7 8 9 10 11 12 13 14 15 / 20 19 18 17 16 15 14 13 12 11 10

Rights for publishing this book outside the U.S.A. or in non-English languages are
administered by Gospel Light Worldwide, an international not-for-profit ministry.
For additional information, please visit www.glww.org, email info@glww.org, or write
to Gospel Light Worldwide, 1957 Eastman Avenue, Ventura, CA 93003, U.S.A.

To order copies of this book and other Regal products in bulk quantities,
please contact us at 1-800-446-7735.

For Cathy—
You continue to amaze me and inspire me.
Thank you for your sacrificial example of making
our family your priority.

Contents

Foreword *by Gary D. Chapman, Ph.D.* 6

Acknowledgments 8

Introduction 9

1. The Power of Being There 12

2. Parenting with Affection, Warmth and Encouragement . . .27

3. Build Healthy Morals and Values .43

4. Discipline with Consistency 66

5. Ruthlessly Eliminate Stress 84

6. Communication Is the Key 101

7. Play Is Necessary for a Close-Knit Family 119

8. Love Your Spouse 132

9. The Best Things in Life Are Not Things 150

10. Energize Your Family's Spiritual Growth 165

Endnotes 184

Foreword

Of all the influences on the maturation process, none is more important than the family. Healthy families tend to produce healthy individuals. Conversely, dysfunctional families tend to produce troubled individuals.

Human development studies in recent years have focused on the dysfunctional family so intently that most people now believe they grew up in one. Most of the people who come into my counseling office say during the first visit, "I grew up in a dysfunctional family." Then they proceed to bring out the tangled wires of their past and seek to make sense of their present. I am deeply sympathetic, and I invest a great deal of my life trying to help them find their way. Yet, in the last few years, I have had a growing awareness that many in our day have no clear picture of a *functional* family. They know the pain and problems of dysfunction, but they do not know what a healthy family looks like.

When your local bank trains employees how to spot counterfeit bills, it does not show them samples of the counterfeit. Instead, it leads them to focus intently on the authentic bills—to study every detail and visualize the image of the true until it is imprinted on the mind. With this mental imprint of the real bill, bank employees are more likely to spot the counterfeit. I believe the same principle applies to helping people develop healthy families. For the past few years, our focus has been on examining the counterfeit—studying the elements of the dysfunctional family. There is benefit in this process, especially in terms of helping those who grew up in such settings, to identify the elements of family relationships that molded their social and emotional patterns. But when there has been some measure of healing, there is the desperate need for a new model. What does a healthy family look like? Until we have a clear picture of a healthy family, we are not likely to create one.

How refreshing to find in the writings of Jim Burns a focus on the real thing. Bringing together contemporary research and biblical foundations, he focuses on those elements of family life that create healthy families. Trained as a professional, he writes in the language of the layman, with an emphasis on the practical. You will not have difficulty understanding the 10 principles of families that succeed—though, admittedly, implementation will require time and effort.

Here is a book that answers the question, *What does a healthy family look like?* It's a book I can recommend enthusiastically.

Gary D. Chapman, Ph.D.
Author of the bestselling *The Five Love Languages*
Winston-Salem, North Carolina

Acknowledgments

Special thanks to:

Cindy Ward
*Cathy and I are blessed by your partnership in ministry
and your incredible friendship.*

Carrie Hicks Steele
*You constantly work far above and beyond the call of duty.
You are a blessing and a gift sent straight from God.*

Christy, Rebecca and Heidi Burns
*You bring me the greatest joy of my life.
What a delight and privilege to be your dad.*

Dr. Jon Wallace
You are an inspirational friend and hero.

David Peck
What a joy to work together to change the world!

The Board of Directors of HomeWord,
*as well as the thousands of supporters and friends who
have helped create this worldwide, grassroots movement
of family-based youth ministry
You are making a difference.*

Kim Bangs
*You are a treasure who makes all with whom you come
in contact feel special. Thanks for being my "go-to" person
at Regal/Gospel Light.*

Introduction

The day our oldest daughter, Christy, arrived home from the hospital, I panicked. *How do I hold her? How do I change her? What do we do with her for the next 50 years?* Today she is a young adult, and I'm still panicked.

Parenting isn't easy. In fact, it is humbling. Parenting has brought out the very best and the very worst in me. If you are having an easy time as a parent, then something is probably wrong. Yes, our children have brought Cathy and me closer together than we ever imagined, and yes, our strongest disagreements have come to us compliments of having children.

Christy Meredith Burns arrived weighing in at 6 pounds and 10 ounces. No one had sent us to parenting school, so we started making up what to do and how to react. The problem was that we came from typical dysfunctional families and found ourselves copying behavior we had actually resented growing up. We decided we needed help. Cathy had a degree in child development and I had one in youth and family ministry, but we were still lost.

So we came up with a great idea. We would look for lessons from mentors. We examined the finest books on family written during the past 25 years. We interviewed hundreds of couples and young people. We dialogued with colleagues. As we explored high and low for the right way to parent, we learned two very important things: (1) there is no perfect method to parenting, and (2) most parents are doing a very adequate job of parenting but don't know it. We also concluded that there are basically 10 essential ingredients for a solid, healthy family. What came out of that search is the content of this simple parenting book.

In my own writing and speaking work, I have focused most often on families and kids in crisis. Sometimes the news media can be extremely negative when it comes to families and children. However, there is some very good news that often gets missed by the newspeople. Thousands upon thousands of families around the world are thriving and working positively through their issues.

Many parents came from dysfunctional homes and inherited some of their parents' problems, but now they're breaking the chain of dysfunction and working hard at parenting their children in a more positive environment—they are the transitional generation for their children. The result will be children who are more secure, and a legacy of love and health will be passed on to the next generation.

Cathy and I will be the first to tell you that no family is perfect. Our three children will be the next to agree that our family has a long way to go, but we're on this journey together. Join us as we look at the 10 building blocks for a solid family.

● ● ●

To measure your progress along the way, there is an opportunity at the end of each chapter to build on what you are learning. The Discussion Starters section contains statements and questions to help you engage with the content, as well as practical tools to assist you in evaluating and improving the happiness and health of your family. HomeWord has also developed an excellent small-group curriculum for parenting groups based on the book. Here's to happy, healthy and solid families!

The 10 Building Blocks for a Solid Family

1. The Power of Being There
Your children regard your very presence as a sign of caring and connectedness.

2. Express Affirmation, Warmth and Encouragement
Parents who practice AWE-based parenting, as opposed to shame-based parenting, will create a home where children and spouses feel more secure.

3. Build Healthy Morals and Values
The decisions kids make today will often affect them for the rest of their lives.

4. Discipline with Consistency
Clearly expressed expectations and consistent follow-through produce responsible kids.

5. Ruthlessly Eliminate Stress
The unbalanced life will not be kind to the areas we neglect.

6. Communication Is the Key
Positive communication is the language of love for our children.

7. Play Is Necessary for a Close-Knit Family
There is nothing like play to bring about family togetherness and communication.

8. Love Your Spouse
A loving marriage brings hope and security to your children.

9. The Best Things in Life Are Not Things
Healthy stewardship and sound financial decisions produce positive family priorities.

10. Energize Your Family's Spiritual Growth
Your greatest calling in life is to leave a spiritual legacy for your children.

1

The Power of Being There

My mom died a few years ago. It wasn't easy. Cancer racked her body, and we spent most of a year watching her die.

We had moved Mom home from the hospital and were trying to make her as comfortable as possible with hospice care. We moved a hospital bed into Mom and Dad's bedroom. I would often find myself sitting on their bed while she lay in her hospital bed.

One day she was dozing and very weak, when all of a sudden she perked up and asked me, "Jimmy, where is your dad?"

"He's watching a baseball game on TV. Do you need him, Mom?"

"No, not really," she replied. Then she looked up at me and said, "You know, Jimmy, I never really liked baseball."

"You never liked baseball, Mom?" I was puzzled. "Did you ever miss a Little League game of mine?"

"No."

"Did you miss any of my Pony League, junior high or high school games, Mom?"

Again she replied, "I don't think so."

"Mom," I continued, "you never missed a game, and on top of that you never missed any of my three brothers' games either. Dad and you watch ball games all day long on TV. What do you mean you never liked baseball?"

"Jimmy, I didn't go to the games to watch baseball. I went to the games to be with you!"

I realized at that moment that this incredible woman had such a powerful impact on my life because she was there, even when she didn't care for the activity. Her very presence in my life was cause for great inspiration and influence. She taught me the power of being there.

• • •

Your children regard your very presence as a sign of caring and connectedness. The power of being there makes a difference in a child's life. This sounds so simple, but don't underestimate the positive message you are giving your kids by watching those games, driving them all around the county or being with them in one of the hundreds of other ways you are present in their lives. You don't have to be present with your kids 24/7, but your presence gives them a greater sense of security than almost anything else you can offer them. All studies on positive family living tell us that the meaningful times families spend together are well worth it. Soccer moms—it's worth it. Dads who leave work early to watch the game—it's worth it. Single parents—as tired as you may be, if you continue to find the time to go on special outings with your kids, you will reap the benefits now and later in your family life.

Here are a few things I have learned about parenting during the past 16 years:

- *Parenting isn't easy.* If you are having an easy go at it, then something is probably wrong. Parenting is exhausting. Just ask the mother of a newborn—or of a 2-year-old, a 10-year-old or even a 16-year-old, for that matter!

- *Parenting is frustrating.* We still live in a make-believe world in which some of us actually expect that there is a place this side of heaven where no conflict resides. If there is such a place, it isn't in the family.

- *Parenting is delayed gratification.* Parents plant seeds in their children that will not sprout until adulthood. Parenting is partnering with God to bring His children into the world and to help them become all they are meant to be.

• *Parenting is the highest calling on earth.* There is no doubt that one of the primary reasons God placed you on this planet was to pass on a positive, healthy legacy to your family.

The crazy thing about parenting is that there is no single method or plan that works perfectly; there is no guarantee that if what you are doing is working with kid number one, it will work with kids number two, three, four or however many kids you are brave enough to have. You can debate the various philosophies of parenting and family life. Believe me, there are hundreds—no, thousands—of parenting plans out there. Many of them actually contradict each other! However, all healthy parenting plans will tell you, in one way or another, that happy, healthy families experience the power of being there for each other. Most parents reading this book are doing a much better job than they think; and although the only evident results are long-term, their investment of time, attention and presence in the lives of their children will make a positive difference.

The Priority of Children

Your job as a parent is a calling from God. It is more important than your vocation, bank account, education or even your own happiness. Besides your relationship with God Himself, your relationship with your children is primary; your influence and impact on them will, no doubt, be your greatest legacy.

Throughout the Bible, family and children are top priorities. Jesus' disagreement with His disciples, recorded in Mark 10:13-16, shows us the heart of God when it comes to children:

People were bringing little children to Jesus to have him touch them, but the disciples rebuked them. When Jesus saw this, he was indignant. He said to them, "Let the little children come to me, and do not hinder them, for the kingdom of God belongs to such as these. I tell you the truth, anyone who will not receive the kingdom of God like a little child will never enter it." And he took the children in his arms, put his hands on them and blessed them.

On another occasion, Jesus was discussing the priority of children with His disciples, but the disciples kept interrupting Him and wanted to talk about "more important" issues. However, Jesus gently kept bringing them back to lessons on children. Look at Mark 9:36-37:

> He [Jesus] took a little child and had him stand among them. Taking him in his arms, he said to them [the disciples], "Whoever welcomes one of these little children in my name welcomes me; and whoever welcomes me does not welcome me but the one who sent me."

When you welcome a child, you welcome Jesus. How's that for priority?

The first time I spoke to people in Guatemala, I met one of the most radiant women I will ever meet. Halfway through the first general session, she appeared in the back of the hall. She wore a colorful Indian skirt, hand-embroidered blouse, beads and a brilliant smile. She was probably about 4 feet 11 inches by 4 feet 11 inches!

I asked my interpreter, Jeffrey DeLeon, "Who is the incredible woman who came in halfway through the first presentation?" I had noticed that he had nodded to her.

He answered, "Oh, she is a saint. She lives in a mountainous section of our country and may be the only person in her area within hundreds of miles who works with children and youth. She probably rode on a bus at least 12 hours—all night—to get here. She is an exceptional woman."

"I want to meet her," I replied. He then told me that her 12-year-old son had died about three months earlier. I asked him, "How does she do it? How does she still manage to work with kids? I think I would be curled up in the fetal position if something like that ever happened to me." He encouraged me to go ask her.

I walked up to her, and we connected even though we didn't know each other's language very well. I said, *"Lo siento"* (I'm sorry). She nodded as if she understood. I then asked in the most broken Spanish known to humankind, "How do you manage to still work with kids when your own son died just three months ago?" She smiled, although there was grief in her eyes, and said, *"Porque los niños están más cerca al corazón de Dios"* (Because children are closer to the heart of God).

When Jesus said, "When you welcome a child, you welcome Me," He was clearly communicating that your role as a parent is a most important calling.

She was right. When Jesus said, "When you welcome a child, you welcome Me," He was clearly communicating that your role as a parent is a most important calling. We can see how close children are to the heart of God when we see Jesus get angry. One of the few times in the Bible we see Jesus' anger is in His response to the wrongful treatment of children. Look at these strong words of Jesus: "And if anyone causes one of these little ones who believe in me to sin, it would be better for him to be thrown into the sea with a large millstone tied around his neck" (Mark 9:42).

We have a friend, Peggy, who chose to be a stay-at-home mom. She is lovely and brilliant, and she sacrificed a great deal of money by choosing to stay at home. Her husband was a professor at a prestigious university on the East Coast. Recently, she told my wife, Cathy, and me that she was always intimidated by faculty social gatherings. People would turn to her and ask, "And what is it that you do, my dear?" At first she would sheepishly say something like, "Oh, I'm just a mom." The response was usually, "Oh, that's nice." That is, until our friend Peggy came up with a new line: "I am socializing two homo sapiens into the dominant values of the Judeo-Christian tradition in order that they might be the instruments for the transformation of the social order into the kind of eschatological utopia that God willed from the beginning of creation!" Peggy's description of parenting reminds us that whether we choose to stay at home with our children or work outside the home, our true vocation is to develop a happy, healthy family; whatever else we do is secondary.

The Blessing of Your Presence

I have the privilege to speak and listen to thousands of young people each year. What do they desire most from their parents? A relationship with them. They seek their parents' time and attention. Please never underestimate the power of being there for your children. The key thought to remember is that you can bless your kids with your very presence.

Bless Your Kids with Your Presence

You are probably already blessing your kids with your presence and doing it well. In reality, moms often do this better than dads. Dads sometimes get sidetracked. My daughter Rebecca reminded me of the power of being there when she was in third grade. One night at dinner she announced to the family that I was coming to Mrs. Saxe's third-grade class for her show-and-tell time. Rebecca hadn't asked; she simply told us. I asked her if the other daddies were being invited to come to class.

She said, "No, Dad, just you."

I replied, "Don't you usually share a book or a doll or pictures?"

She answered, "Usually, Dad, but not on Tuesday. I promised my teacher you would come."

"What if I can't come that day?"

"Then you'll need to change your schedule. I promised my teacher!"

"Rebecca, do you want me to bring my résumé?"

"What's a résumé?"

"It lists all the important things mommies and daddies do."

"No, don't bring that. I'd be embarrassed."

"Do you want me to bring the book I wrote and dedicated to you?"

"No, Dad. Don't bring the book. Just relax and bring yourself!"

So I agreed to go to her class, without anything to impress her fellow third graders.

On that Tuesday, I spoke to 3,500 high school students at an assembly on drug and alcohol abuse. No problem. That's what I'm comfortable doing. But as I drove to Rebecca's class, I grew more and more nervous. Would the kids like me? I didn't want to embarrass Rebecca. What could I say to a bunch of third graders? I arrived at her school a bit early and walked to Rebecca's class. I figured I would sit in the back and get comfortable with the kids while Mrs. Saxe was teaching the class.

As I opened the door, every eye turned toward me and away from Mrs. Saxe, who was teaching math. She pointed for me to go the back of the room and wait. (I had been sent to the back of the room when I was in school, but for a different reason!) While Mrs. Saxe continued teaching, Rebecca interrupted the class by standing up, walking over to me, taking my hand and saying, "Come on, Dad. It's your turn." I tried to whisper that Mrs. Saxe was not ready for me, but it didn't matter to Rebecca. She pulled me to the front of the class, pushing Mrs. Saxe out of the way. The teacher smiled and reluctantly canceled the remainder of the math lesson for the day.

Rebecca introduced me to the class. "This is my dad. His name is Jim. He is a great guy and he's bald" (as if they hadn't noticed!).

I spoke for five minutes and then made a beeline for the door. Mrs. Saxe stopped me and said, "Dr. Burns, perhaps some of the children have questions for you." I'm thinking, *Right, third graders have questions for me?* Dozens of hands shot up. I pointed to Matthew. "Do you have a question, Matt?"

"Yeah, how old are you anyway? You look kind of old to be Rebecca's dad."

With my self-esteem sinking, I told him my age. He just shook his head. I had never thought of myself as old until that moment! I needed encouragement, so I turned to Rebecca's good friend Mallory. "Yes, Mallory?"

"Jim," she began, letting the rest of the kids know that we were on a first-name basis, "do you own a dog?"

"Well, uh, Mallory, of course, you know that we, uh, do not own a dog." I was caught in a setup, and it didn't matter that I proceeded to tell the class that we had other animals.

Mallory looked around the room for support and shouted back, "Rebecca wants a dog!" My self-esteem continued to sink. (Incidentally, today Rebecca has a beautiful golden retriever that I feed, walk and clean up after.) The questions continued one after another. None of the kids asked about my educational background or salary or any of the other things that we adults often place on the pedestal of importance. The kids mainly asked relational questions.

Most often, the difference between kids who make it and kids who don't is one caring adult.

When I finally finished answering the last question, again I headed for the door. This time Rebecca stood up and came toward me. I thought, *Oh, no. What now?* She reached her arms around me with a big hug and simply said, "Daddy, thank you for coming to class today. I am so proud of you."

Rebecca and her third-grade class didn't see my tears, but I cried all the way to my car. It had dawned on me that Rebecca doesn't care about academic degrees, awards, credentials or even money (although she wouldn't mind more gas money for her car right now); she cares about relationships. She wants my time and attention and my presence. Her security does not come from my work; it comes from my presence. Our children crave our presence, and nothing can make up for our absence.

Presence Matters

Another important ingredient in parenting is *expressing your belief in your kids.* Most young people struggle with a poor or improper self-image. They play the comparison game and see that some-one is always smarter, prettier, more coordinated or richer than they are. They need someone in their lives who believes in them, even when they can't believe in themselves. Don't forget this: *Most often the difference between kids who make it and kids who don't is one caring adult.*

Jesus met a fisherman named Simon, and early in their rela-tionship He nicknamed him *Petras* (Peter). "Petras" means "rock." Yes, Jesus nicknamed him Rocky. Jesus even made a wordplay with Peter's name when He pointed to Simon Peter and said, "On this rock I will build my church" (Matt. 16:18). Who became the leader of the Early Church? It was Simon, the stumbling, bum-bling fisherman who became Peter, the rock-solid leader of the Church—and that transformation began with Jesus' ability to see in Simon what Simon could not see in himself. Parents should pray for the same ability that Jesus had, so that they may believe in their children and help build up their shaky self-images to be-come all God has in store for them to be.

Next, you must *shower your children with praise.* Mark Twain is known to have said, "I can live for two months on a good compli-ment." It is attributed to Abraham Maslow, the great Jewish thinker, to have said that for every critical statement we make about another person, we must speak nine affirming statements to make up for it. Praise and affirmation are positive, motivating factors. Put-downs are deflating.

Praise your kids, but don't lie to them—there is a difference. If my parents had told me that I was the best-looking boy at Fre-mont Junior High, I would have known they were lying! The next time they praised me, I would have questioned their sincerity. Vain flattery is an emotional withdrawal, but true, meaningful praise will be a major deposit into your children's emotional bank accounts. Praise your children often, and praise their inner as well as outer qualities.

Next, *be available.* It's back to the power of being there for your kids. A recent study on kids who are prone to drug and alcohol abuse showed that if a family has dinner together several nights a week, their children will be less likely to be involved in drug or alcohol abuse.[1] Your very presence in their lives makes a difference.

Nene, my grandma, was one of the major heroes of my life. At 87, she was deteriorating physically and mentally due to Alzheimer's disease. Sometimes she recognized me and sometimes she didn't. I never dreamed she would live to see the birth of our last child, but she did. She was even able to come to the baby shower. I have a picture of Nene holding our youngest daughter, Heidi, and I treasure that picture to this day.

*When kids understand that their parents
are there for them, they can overcome
amazing obstacles and circumstances to make a
positive impact in their world.*

When it was time to open the presents at our baby shower, my brother Bill went over to help Nene out of her chair. I happened to be walking by when he said, "Come on, Nene, let's go watch Jim and Cathy open those gifts for their new baby, Heidi."

Dazed and confused, she said, "Who?"

He shouted in her ear (she was also hearing impaired), "Jim and Cathy have a new baby, and we are going to open some gifts. Come on, I'll help you up."

Frustrated and in pain, she told Bill, "I can't get up. I didn't buy them a present. I'm tired, I'm old and I just want to die."

Bill gently replied, "Nene, I don't think anyone is concerned that you didn't purchase a gift."

At that point I walked up to my dear, loving grandma and said, "Nene, your very presence in the room makes a difference to me. For all my life, just your presence has given me strength."

Nene died shortly after the baby shower. She never really had much money, but that did not matter to me. It wasn't her gifts that made a difference in my life; it was her presence and availability that still give me strength today.

The Power of Your Presence

The power of being there for our children is so profoundly meaningful that we often miss it. When kids understand that their parents are there for them, they can overcome amazing obstacles and circumstances to make a positive impact in their world. The power of being there is a deposit into a child's emotional, physical and spiritual bank account that will pay off in dividends of intimacy and understanding in a family. Many times parents look for the latest parenting fad to help their families become close-knit. Yet the answer is simple and right in front of them: investing your time, energy and commitment to be there for your children. The result is hope and security for all.

In 1989, an earthquake in what was then Soviet Armenia took only four minutes to flatten the nation and kill more than 30,000 people. Here's how Max Lucado described one moving scene from this horrible disaster:

> Moments after the deadly tremor ceased, a father raced to an elementary school to save his son. When he arrived, he saw that the building had been leveled. Looking at the mass of stones and rubble, he remembered a promise he had made to his child: "No matter what happens, I'll always be there for you." Driven by his own promise, he found the area closest to his son's room and began to pull back the rocks. Other parents arrived and began sobbing for their children. "It's too late," they told the man. "You know they are dead. You can't help." Even a police officer encouraged him to give up.
>
> But the father refused. For eight hours, then sixteen, then thirty-two—for thirty-six hours he dug. His hands were raw and his energy gone, but he refused to quit. Finally, after thirty-eight wrenching hours, he pulled back a boulder and heard his son's voice. He called his boy's name, "Arman! Arman!" And a voice answered him, "Dad, it's me!" The boy added these priceless words, "I told the other kids not to worry. I told them if you were alive, you'd

save me, and when you saved me, they'd be saved, too. Because you promised me, 'No matter what I'll always be there for you.'"[2]

DISCUSSION STARTERS

1. When you were a child, did you experience the power of being there from your parents?

_____

_____

_____

_____

_____

2. Use the following scale to rate your own parenting with your child/children:

The Power of Your Presence

1	2	3	4	5
needs attention		so-so		great

3. "Your children regard your very presence as a sign of caring and connectedness." How do you interpret this statement?

_____

_____

_____

_____

_____

4. What do you see as the significant message of Jesus' words and actions in the following verses?

People were bringing little children to Jesus to have him touch them, but the disciples rebuked them. When Jesus saw this, he was indignant. He said to them, "Let the little children come to me, and do not hinder them, for the kingdom of God belongs to such as these. I tell you the truth, anyone who will not receive the kingdom of God like a little child will never enter it." And he took the children in his arms, put his hands on them and blessed them (Mark 10:13-16).

He took a little child and had him stand among them. Taking him in his arms, he said to them, "Whoever welcomes one of these little children in my name welcomes me; and whoever welcomes me does not welcome me but the one who sent me" (Mark 9:36-37).

And if anyone causes one of these little ones who believe in me to sin, it would be better for him to be thrown into the sea with a large millstone tied around his neck (Mark 9:42).

_____

_____

_____

_____

_____

_____

_____

_____

_____

5. Jesus believed in the bigmouthed fisherman, who later became the leader of the Early Church. Read the following Scriptures, keeping in mind that both *Cephas* (Aramaic) and *Petras* (Greek) mean "rock"; and consider these questions:

What can you do to believe in your child more? Who is the Simon Peter in your life right now?

And he [Andrew] brought him [Simon] to Jesus. Jesus looked at him and said, "You are Simon son of John. You will be called Cephas" (which, when translated, is Peter) (John 1:42).

And I tell you that you are Peter [Petras], and on this rock I will build my church, and the gates of Hades will not overcome it (Matt. 16:18).

_____

_____

_____

_____

_____

_____

_____

_____

Practical Ideas for Spending Time with Your Children

Here's a list created by children ages 6 to 18 of activities they would like to do with their parent or parents:

1. Make daily phone calls
2. Plan weekly dates
3. Establish special traditions
4. Attend their games and plays
5. Drive them to school
6. Put together puzzles
7. Watch a special TV program and eat popcorn
8. Write them notes
9. Take them on a business trip
10. Take photography lessons together
11. Play tennis
12. Skip rocks and have a contest
13. Write a letter to God
14. Walk the dog
15. Read a good book together
16. Go out for breakfast or doughnuts
17. Take pictures
18. Go to the park
19. Visit the library and ask the librarian a bizarre question
20. Develop a new laugh together
21. Visit the zoo
22. Visit a museum
23. Ride bikes
24. Learn a hobby
25. Wash a car
26. Rollerblade
27. Climb a tree
28. Climb a mountain
29. Eat creatively one whole day for $1.29
30. Picnic
31. Shop for cars
32. Go to the airport and watch people
33. Visit the beach or lake
34. Ice-skate
35. Shop
36. Play backgammon
37. Go horseback riding
38. Play pinball
39. Hit golf balls or play some miniature golf
40. Bowl
41. Play water sports
42. Fly a kite
43. Go on a hike
44. Plant a garden together
45. Play board games or card games
46. Fish
47. Sail
48. Play tennis
49. Play croquet
50. Go river rafting or tubing
51. Play badminton
52. Build a tree house
53. Go to a casual dinner but dress up
54. Make homemade ice cream
55. Bake cookies
56. Attend a play
57. Go to the movies
58. Go to a sports event
59. Visit a swap meet or a garage sale
60. Feed ducks
61. Go to the circus
62. Go to the county fair
63. Volunteer at a soup kitchen

Take a moment with your child and create your own list of activities for the next month. Whenever possible, allow your child to offer up the ideas, because children support what they help create.

2

Parenting with Affection, Warmth and Encouragement

I didn't meet Rob Thibaut until he was 43, and he died when he was 50. Many men don't have what you would call a best friend; but from the first time I met Rob, he took over a major place in my heart. We met in Maui at a church where I was speaking. He handed me his business card and asked if we could meet to talk about his relationship with his daughter. Our family was in Hawaii on a three-month sabbatical, and I almost turned him down; but something told me that it would be a special meeting. It was.

I counseled him, but somehow this man gave me an amazing amount of strength and energy. We continued to meet while I was in Maui—sometimes socially and sometimes to talk over family issues. What makes this guy tick? I wondered.

After my first meeting with Rob, I pulled out his business card. He was the president of a successful restaurant chain in Hawaii and California, which soon became my favorite. He told me later that he was on former President Gerald Ford's foundation board. I was amazed by how many movie stars he knew, and I could only imagine that his bank account was quite comfortable. Usually people like him intimidated me, but Rob didn't. He poured the same amount of love and energy into the dishwashers at his restaurant as he did into the ex-presidents of the United States whom he knew.

He rapidly moved from counselee to friend, mentor and teacher. What is it about this man? I asked myself.

It wasn't until one night after my family had returned home that I figured it out. I "happened" to be in Maui before flying to Honolulu to speak at a conference. On my voice mail at the hotel, I had a message from Rob, whom I planned to see the next day. He said, "Jimmy, I can't meet with you tomorrow. I'm in the hospital, and the doctor just told me I don't have long to live. I'm worried about Patty and the kids. Will you check in with them for me? I love you, and aloha, Jim." I sat on the edge of my bed in the hotel room stunned, and then I literally ran to my car to drive to the other side of the island to sit with Rob at the hospital. His wife, Patty, had just left for the night, and Rob was all alone.

We talked for two hours about his love for his beautiful wife and his three incredible kids. He shared about each child one at a time and told me his favorite family stories. Almost like the prophets of the Old Testament, he blessed his children one by one. We talked about his dad, his work, his friends and his faith. I read Scriptures to him. That night, Rob and I prayed together, held each other and cried.

A week later Cathy and I sat at Rob's funeral, or more appropriately, celebration. It was a mix of Hawaiian hula and song, strong Christian testimony, and a lovely tribute to a wonderful husband, father and friend. As we all boarded boats near his beloved Napili Bay, Maui, to pay our respects, it finally hit me: Rob treated all people in his presence as if they were special guests at a party in their honor. He didn't complain or nag or whine about life. Sure, he was a realist, but he validated our worth through a positive spirit, even when he knew he was dying. He was a great man who empowered people through affirmation, warmth and encouragement.

If the love and respect we gather in a lifetime is the measure of a man, then Rob was a great man. He was a positive encouragement to so many people. He always had time for each individual and made everyone feel special. Rob had close relationships—either as best friend, best man, mentor, parent or husband—with at least half of the people who attended his fiftieth-birthday bash, which occurred a few months before he died. He was the most generous and loving man I have ever known. I miss you, Rob.

• • •

Tanya struggled in her role as a parent. It wasn't because she didn't love her kids or failed to put in the effort. If anything, Tanya tried too hard and expected more from herself as a parent than was humanly possible to achieve. Her relationship with her husband, Paul, was suffering, partly due to the fact that she was exhausted from expending so much energy on the all-consuming role of mother. She told me once that one of her boys said, "You think you are a good mommy, but you really aren't." Ouch! Yet there might have been a hint of truth in that statement, not because she neglected her boys—far from it—but because she had no life besides her children. She was using the same dysfunctional parenting philosophy her dysfunctional parents used with her.

Tanya didn't come from an Ozzie and Harriet family. Her mom was pregnant with her at age 17, and her dad was forced into a shotgun wedding. Her grandma struggled emotionally, her mom struggled with depression, and now she struggled—period. Coming from a dysfunctional home, Tanya battled a low self-image and an extremely negative spirit, which she unleashed regularly on her boys and her husband. We met together because she sensed that things were spiraling more and more out of control with her teenage son; she wanted insight about him. Tanya also mentioned that she and her husband were really at odds with each other but that they didn't have the emotional strength to work on the marriage.

I asked the whole family to come in so that we could get acquainted. Quickly, the session went sour when everyone ganged up on Tanya. She was "too controlling," "too negative," "inconsistent with discipline"—nag, nag, nag. Tanya had tears in her eyes. She had learned to be a pretty tough character, and because of her unhealthy family background, her response was to get defensive. She fought back. In a very controlled manner she told me each of the children's bad sides and took her husband to task for lots of little issues—and I'm sure what she said was mostly true. The family went silent. Tanya had won the battle. Her husband and children were embarrassed and shamed by her criticism.

Tanya had won the battle, but she was losing the war. Why? Shame-based parenting—when parents attempt to influence their children's behavior by shaming them—simply does not work in the long run. Tanya's grandma had tried shame-based parenting on her mother, her mom had used it as the primary way to communicate with Tanya, and now she used it on her family. It hadn't worked for the previous generations, and it was not working in Tanya's family.

In a later conversation with Tanya, very much aware of her fragile self-image, I said, "At the risk of doing a bit of damage to our friendship, let me say that nagging, overcontrol, negativity and shame-based parenting will get you the initial victory; but unless you make some serious changes and decisions, your relationship with your children is headed down the same path as your relationships with your mother and grandmother. Tanya, are you willing to work as hard as you have ever worked to reestablish and restructure your style of parenting with your kids and the way you relate to your husband?"

She didn't answer my question; instead, she was hurting so badly she decided to tell me a few more zingers about her children and husband. I said, "Did you hear what you just did? You didn't answer my question; you gave out more ammunition to let me know how hard it is being married to Paul and how difficult your kids are. You've convinced me they are challenging. But what about you?" Tanya began to cry.

Tragically, shame-based parenting has been the most dominant style of parenting for the past several centuries. It hasn't worked for our families, but for some reason, we still use and abuse it. If you grew up in a home like Tanya's, you may be asking, "Fine, but what parenting strategy *does* work?"

Parenting with AWE

Cathy and I were able to introduce Tanya to a different style of parenting and, frankly, of relating to people in general. We call it parenting with AWE. "AWE" stands for "affection, warmth and encouragement." Of course, this is easier said than done when we are in the midst of the battle and feel that we're losing ground. It is amazingly easy to revert to the old ways of shame-based parenting since many of its results are immediately evident, while the results of parenting with AWE often only come after a long period of investment.

Many parenting experts talk about a child's "emotional bank account." Using this analogy, shame-based parenting makes many more withdrawals than deposits. Although this may sound like an oversimplification, shame-based parenting focuses on making withdrawals, while AWE-based parenting concentrates on placing deposits into the emotional bank account.

Shame-based parenting focuses on making withdrawals, while AWE-based parenting concentrates on placing deposits into the emotional bank account.

We can also make deposits into and withdrawals from the emotional bank account of our spouse. Joe White, president of Kanakuk-Kanakomo Kamps and an all-around great guy, did something that I'll never forget at a Promise Keepers event. He threw a bag of red beans and a bag of white beans into the arena and challenged the men to try an experiment for a month: Every time they took a withdrawal from their wife's emotional bank account, they should put a red bean in a jar; and every time they made a deposit, they should place a white bean in another jar. After a month, they were to look at the jars and measure how they had done.

Shame-based parenting uses words and actions that cause kids to think they aren't loved or valuable. Shame-based parenting is performance-oriented and approval-focused. Kids from shame-based homes say that nothing was ever good enough for Dad or that Mom used to say things like "Can't you do anything right?" and "Just let me do it, so it gets done on time." Those words win the battle but lose the war.

AWE-based parenting, on the other hand, makes our children feel loved and accepted even in the midst of discipline. I have a plaque hanging on the wall in my office, and I love what it says: "Every child needs someone who is irrationally positive about them." Kids who live in an environment of affection, warmth and encouragement feel listened to and appreciated. These kids have the confidence to go out and take on life because they know their parents believe in them, value them and enjoy them.

Cathy and I need a lot of reminders to drop the old style and pick up the right way to parent. Here's our AWE reminder list:

Deposits
- Saying "I'm sorry" to my children when I blow it
- Praising often
- Believing the best of them
- Forgiving them
- Hugging often
- Saying "I love you" every day
- Writing thank-you notes and love notes
- Praying for them
- Speaking with a tender tone of voice
- Bragging about them
- Playing together
- Listening to them (listening is the language of love)
- Spending time together
- Going out on special dates

Withdrawals
- Nagging
- Belittling them
- Being sarcastic
- Making negative put-downs
- Criticizing
- Screaming
- Never saying "I'm sorry"
- Fighting constantly with my spouse
- Talking about them negatively to others
- Showing favoritism
- Being silent
- Heaping guilt on them
- Being rude and irritable

Parenting with AWE means parenting with affection, warmth and encouragement. It doesn't mean we stop disciplining, but it does mean we try our best to stop shaming our children into making the right decisions. If we would only work as hard at creating a warm, loving environment of affection and affirmation in our family as we do at working in our vocation, we would have a better family atmosphere.

Expressing Affection

Researchers tell us that we need 8 to 10 meaningful touches a day to thrive. Many children—and adults, for that matter—are starved for healthy, positive, appropriate physical attention. Dr. Ross Campbell claims, "In all my research and experience I have never known of one sexually disoriented person who had a warm, loving and affectionate father."[1]

The power of being there is more than just our presence; it is also our touch and affection. Do your kids know you love them? Of course they do. But they still need a hug and a verbal "I love you" on a daily basis. If you didn't come from a family that displayed affection, then you might have more difficulty being affectionate, but your children still need the reassurance and blessing of your affection.

I once wrote a book to students on the topic of sex and dating. Immediately the calls started coming in, usually from mothers who were nervous about their children. They wanted me to meet with their teenagers and fix any problem they were having with their sexuality and relationships. This, of course, was ludicrous; but during that season of my life I met some of the most persistent parents in the world. One mother of a 17-year-old sexually promiscuous daughter called at least 20 times, and my assistant finally pleaded with me to take the appointment so that she could quit spending so much time on the phone with this mother.

On the day of their appointment, we were all a bit curious to see what was going to happen. I must admit how surprised I was to meet two of the nicest parents I had ever met and a beautiful girl with a very pleasing personality. Through our conversation, I confirmed that the girl had become quite sexually active. She was a Christian and felt some remorse, but I really couldn't get to the core of the issue. I asked the mom and dad to step out of my office because I wanted to talk with the daughter by herself. She was pleasant and willing to talk, but she didn't want to talk about her sexuality. She wanted to talk about her father.

Children need to experience touch and affection from their parents, or they will look for a counterfeit as they get older. Touch is a major form of blessing. There is power in touch.

She said, "I used to be so close to my dad. When I was younger, he would play with me and toss me in the air. I would snuggle on his lap, and he would read to me and do magic tricks. When he would come home from work, he would always give me a hug and say 'How's my little princess?'" Then her lip began to quiver, and she looked away from me, saying, "I guess I'm not his little princess anymore."

I had heard enough. I brought the mom and the dad back into the room. I asked the dad, "How's your relationship with your daughter?" He looked over at her with obvious love and the first hint of tenderness I had seen from him and said, "We used to be close. I would play with her and read to her and pick her up in the air and call her my little princess." Now it was his turn for his lip to quiver. Maybe it was hereditary! He looked at me and added, "Then when she got to be about 13, her body started changing, as well as her attitude, and it was just more difficult."

I looked him right in the eyes and said, "My friend, if you don't take the time to hug your daughter with appropriate hugs often, there are hundreds of boys who would love to hug her with inappropriate hugs and more." She needed to be his little princess now more than ever.

Children need to experience touch and affection from their parents, or they will look for a counterfeit as they get older. Jesus took the little children in His arms and blessed them. Touch is a major form of blessing. In the Bible, when parents blessed a child, they very often placed loving hands on the child and embraced them. There is power in touch. If you come from a home in which you did not receive much affection or touch, then it may be difficult for you to pour on the affection. You don't need to move from stoic to mushy, but there is a happy medium that may require you to stretch your comfort level for the sake of your children.

After a seminar, one man told me, "You just don't understand how difficult it is for me to hold my three children. I grew up in a home where my very formal parents never hugged us kids. My dad showed his love by working hard and bringing home an excellent paycheck, and my mom showered her love on us with wonderful home-cooked meals." I think he was looking for me to excuse him.

I replied, "I'm very sorry that you did not receive the power of physical touch in your home growing up, and yet it sounds like you came from a home where your parents did the best they could do." He nodded in agreement.

I continued, "Now you can be the transitional generation and pass on to your children the love you received from your parents *and* the power of touch. No one said parenting would be easy, but you now know better. It will get easier."

His wife smiled and said, "He's going to need quite a bit of practice."

"Great," I agreed. Turning back toward the man, I said, "It sounds like you have three little ones you can 'practice' with and probably your wife could use a hug more often also." His wife nodded in agreement. I'd bet everyone in his family received a hug that day.

Creating Warmth

For your family to have a sense of AWE, *create a home environment of warmth and affection.* You may be saying, "But you don't understand what my spouse is like" or "My adolescent isn't exactly the perfect example of love, affection and devotion." I'm sure you're right; so start by taking "baby steps" (as Bill Murray's character in the hilarious movie *What About Bob?* would say).

Taking baby steps means that if you have 20 things to go over with your teenager when he or she gets home from school and most of the agenda deals with things your teenager should have done but didn't—wait. Instead, join your teen in one of youth's favorite pastimes—hanging out. Take your child out for his or her favorite junk food. Don't bring up anything on your agenda; instead, spend your time listening to whatever your child wants to talk about. Ask no probing questions; make no accusations. Talk with your child the way his or her friends, youth pastor or favorite relative would talk with him or her. Your child will be waiting for the other shoe to drop, but bite your tongue and don't drop the shoe! Keep the conversation warm and friendly. When you are finished, give your child a hug and tell him or her how much you enjoyed being together. You still have those 20 things on your agenda, don't you? So now, after some hang-out time, ask your child when would be a good time to go over some responsibilities. You'll usually get a better reception.

Terri was one of those type-A moms who accomplished more in one day than I could in one week. She was so driven that her children and husband were beginning to find ways to avoid her. Her daughter complained to me that although her mom meant well, almost every night, when the daughter was tired and getting ready for bed, her mom would start with 20 questions, school problems and whatever else was on her list. Usually the conversation would turn into a fight, with doors slamming and words spoken that they both later regretted.

The young girl told me, "My mom greets me at the door after school with a to-do list and doesn't give me a break until I go to sleep. Sometimes I fake like I'm sleeping because I don't want Mom to ask me another question or challenge me with one more problem."

I knew Terri and knew that she wasn't the wicked witch of the west, but I concluded that she probably was developing an unhealthy parenting habit. I suggested to Terri that she not greet her daughter with a to-do list and definitely not follow her around as she was getting ready for bed. They both would be much better off if Terri greeted her daughter with warmth and affection and then made sure that the last event of the day also centered on warmth and affection. The daughter would need to have a specific time each day for Terri to check her homework and make sure "the list" was taken care of. With this routine, Mom's agenda would be handled and the daughter would feel the warmth and affection of a beautiful relationship.

If I were sitting with your child and spouse, how would they rate the warmth of your home? No one is looking for a fake sense of peace; but happy, healthy families work on creating a positive, warm environment even in the midst of disciplining and living out daily life.

Giving Encouragement

When you encourage your children and your spouse, you have the unique ability to *make them feel special. Parakaleo,* the New Testament Greek word for "encourage," or "exhort," can also be translated "call to one's side," "strengthen," "instruct" and "teach."[2] Exhortation is not just about positive reinforcement and encouragement; it is also about challenging your children and spouse to be all they were created by God to be. Your life and words speak into their lives with comfort, counsel, affirmation and challenge.

To encourage your children, you also will want to *set realistic expectations for them.* Many kids suffer from a very poor self-image. They play the comparison game and lose every single time. When it comes to brains, beauty and bucks, our society is not kind to this generation of young people. If we aren't careful, we as parents will reinforce the unrealistic cultural expectations that confront our children daily.

A couple came into my office very upset about their teenage daughter, who had decided to be influenced by the punk-rock culture. Her hair was dyed stark white. Every piece of clothing she was wearing was black; and her makeup definitely made the statement "I don't want to be like my parents," who, as successful businesspeople, dressed very conservatively. Their daughter seemed nice enough, but even as a youth worker who had seen it all, I thought she looked Halloweenish. I thought, *I'm glad my daughters don't look like her.*

As the parents began to talk about their daughter, they were very tough on her, expressing lofty goals that she was never going to achieve—at least not in her current frame of mind. Her parents, both Stanford University graduates, expected her to be getting straight As and following in their footsteps. They kept saying that when she was younger, she had never received even one B and that she didn't understand that success was spelled Stanford, As, business and a new hairstyle! As a parent, I could understand their concerns somewhat, but I still felt uneasy. The daughter was very polite the entire time her parents unfolded their plan for her life. Now it was her turn.

Her parents probably thought I asked a weird question when I turned to the daughter and asked, "So what excites you about life besides rock music?" She paused, smiled and said, "Art."

"Art?" I repeated, surprised.

"Yeah, art. When I was little, Mom would take me to museums, and I fell in love with art. I love music—just not their kind. I love impressionistic painting. I love drama. I would like to work on Broadway as either an actor or artist."

To be honest, I didn't expect what I heard. I expected a caustic teenager, rebellious and self-centered. What I heard behind her purple eyeliner and bright red lipstick was a very articulate, well-educated, enthusiastic young lady with a passion for art and theater.

Now I had a dilemma. I didn't especially like her style of dress, but what she said made sense. She loved her parents but didn't want to grow up to be like them. She had a flair for the artistic side of life, and they had a flair for business. Her parents wanted her to have a Stanford business degree with straight As, but she wanted to study at a college that had a wonderful performing-arts program. If her parents continued to push her to study business at Stanford, they

were setting themselves up for a colossal failure. If she totally re-
belled against her parents' values and relationship, she would be
flirting with disaster. They needed some good old-fashioned negotiation and compromise.

---

*Remember that encouraging means
coming alongside your children and helping them
be all God created them to be.*

We took out a blank piece of paper on which the parents and
daughter negotiated a new set of expectations: "We will drop our
expectation of a Stanford business degree if you will go to class, do
your homework and try your best to get into the school of your
choice. We'll quit nagging you about your clothing under the condition that you wear something besides black every day." Before
the meeting was over, they had in writing a new set of expectations
that both parents and daughter could live with and dialog about.

The question in my mind when they left my office was, *Will
these parents be able to encourage their daughter to excel in her areas of interest?* The answer is that they absolutely did encourage her. They
call that meeting their "parenting conversion." Their daughter
didn't become an *A* student, but she didn't become a dropout either. She threw away her punk-rock outfits—though she still
doesn't own a business suit—and today, their daughter is a vibrant,
talented young actress with a deep Christian commitment.

What are your expectations for your child—whether age 4, 11 or
16—that may not be appropriate? What expectations are acceptable, healthy and worthy of your time and energy? Don't forget to
set the bar of success for your kids. Not every child is an *A* student,
and not all will be captain of the team or get the leading role in the
play. However, every child needs to know that he or she is loved and
believed in. Don't fight every battle—only the absolutely necessary
ones—and remember that encouraging means coming alongside
your children and helping them be all God created them to be.

At the beginning of this chapter, I shared about my friend Rob Thibaut, one of the most wonderful people I've ever known. It was from him that I learned the lesson of this chapter.

Rob's grown daughter, Angela, lived in a different state, so they talked regularly on the phone. When they talked, he always had an agenda; he would say hi and then get right to business. One day he changed his normal procedure: He called Angela and didn't go through any agenda. They talked about a ski trip she had taken. They talked about boys, the weather and a TV program. After 20 minutes, he told Angela he loved her and said goodbye. She called him back 10 minutes later and said, "I just called to say thanks for taking the time out of your busy schedule to call me. I love you." She responded to his genuine interest and care.

I asked Rob, "So when did you get through your list for Angela?"

He smiled and said, "I got two of my main issues dealt with on her return phone call!"

So what's the point? Deal with the issues of the family by *first* creating times of affection, warmth and encouragement. Then your children may be more receptive to doing family business.

● ● ●

For more information on parenting with AWE, check out www.home word.com. It's filled with hundreds of practical helps for parents, students and youth workers. You can search for articles on particular topics, download free articles and sign up to receive our free parenting newsletter by email.

DISCUSSION STARTERS

1. Did you grow up in a family that used shame-based parenting or AWE-based parenting? How did it affect you?

_____

_____

_____

_____

_____

_____

_____

_____

2. What specific steps can you take to enhance an environment of AWE in your family? What often makes it difficult to take these steps?

_____

_____

_____

_____

_____

_____

_____

3. "Every child needs someone who is irrationally positive about them." Did you have that person in your life? Who is or can become that person in the lives of your children?

_____

_____

_____

_____

_____

_____

_____

Positive Deposits You Can Make in Your Child's Life

In the space below, make a list of positive deposits that you can make in your child's life during the next month. As you write out what the deposits will be, make a mark beside each one as to whether it will be Affection, Warmth or Encouragement. Obviously, some of the activities will be more than one of the words from the acronym A.W.E., so mark as many as are applicable.

A W E Deposit

1. __ __ __ _____

2. __ __ __ _____

3. __ __ __ _____

4. __ __ __ _____

5. __ __ __ _____

6. __ __ __ _____

7. __ __ __ _____

8. __ __ __ _____

9. __ __ __ _____

10. __ __ __ _____

11. __ __ __ _____

12. __ __ __ _____

13. __ __ __ _____

14. __ __ __ _____

15. __ __ __ _____

16. __ __ __ _____

17. __ __ __ _____

18. __ __ __ _____

19. __ __ __ _____

20. __ __ __ _____

3

Build Healthy Morals and Values

At one point during the game, the coach said to one of his young players, "Do you understand what cooperation is and what teamwork is all about?" The little boy nodded in the affirmative.

"Do you understand that what really matters is not whether we win or lose but that we play together as a team?" The little boy nodded yes.

"Good," the coach continued. "And when a strike is called or you're thrown out at first, you don't argue, curse, attack the umpire with a bat or throw dirt in the opposing team member's face. Do you understand all that?" Again the little boy nodded. "Well sure, Coach. That's what you taught us."

"Good," said the coach. "Now, please go over there and explain all that to your mother!"

—Told by a friend

• • •

Parenting in Today's Youth Culture

I looked out at an audience of 16-year-old students and began my talk by making this statement: "I'm very glad I'm not 16 years old right now. It's more difficult to grow up today than it was way back when I was 16." Let's face it, as parents we were once 4 years of age and 8, 11 and 16—but we were also never their age, because today's children experience so much so young.

Sure, we had to deal with peer pressure and sexual temptations. Your parents probably griped to you about your choice of music and your choice of language. Students took drugs in your day, and most young boys sneaked a look at *Playboy*. However, we still were never their age.

Today, children can type in one word on the Internet and be exposed to more blatant pornography than you even thought existed back in the good old days.

For the previous generation, the average age for a child or teenager to first taste alcohol was 15; today it is 12.[1] Today, children can type in one word on the Internet and be exposed to more blatant pornography than you even thought existed back in the good old days. A friend recently told me that the average junior higher today is exposed to more sexually explicit innuendos on the way to and from school than my friend had been throughout his entire teenage years. My friend may be right! The average young person can watch more than 14,000 acts of intercourse or innuendo on prime-time TV each year, and the media is getting more brazen and extreme in every avenue of exposure.[2]

Kids and Decision Making

Kids are receiving mixed messages when it comes to morals and values. Let's take sexuality, for example. From home they hear, "Don't do *it*" but not much more about the subject. From church (although it is hopefully changing for the better), they often hear either silence or "Don't do *it* because *it's* dirty, rotten and ugly." From the secular media they often hear, "Do *it*." The secular media is thrilled to sing, write and make movies about sexual promiscuity. When it comes to issues like drugs, sex and rock 'n' roll, kids today are much more influenced by the secular media than by their parents.

At least three factors are involved in the decisions that kids are making about sex, drugs and music. They are important for parents to be aware of and to be prepared to respond to in a proactive manner.

Peer pressure. Peer pressure is one of the most powerful forces affecting kids of all ages. If your children's friends experiment with marijuana or pornography, then the odds are high that your children will, too. The first time I took a sip of alcohol, I was 13. I was at a party where there was alcohol, and though I had already decided I wouldn't drink, my desire to be accepted by my friends was much greater than my desire not to drink.

Emotional involvement that exceeds their maturity level. Kids are making decisions based on emotional involvement that exceeds their maturity level. For example, a 14-year-old girl with a poor self-image who is in love with a sexually promiscuous older guy is very easy to seduce. Her emotional involvement and desire to be liked by the guy are far stronger than the morals she may have learned from home, church or school. She gives in to temptation, not because she's a bad kid, but simply because no one ever helped her learn how to say no. If you have a late bloomer in your home, then get down on your knees and thank God. The decisions kids are making about morals and values today can and do affect them for life.

Just in case you think that dating at an early age is okay, look at these facts:

Age of Dating	Percent Who Have Sex Before Graduation
12 Years	91 percent
13 Years	56 percent
14 Years	53 percent
15 Years	40 percent
16 Years	20 percent[3]

Lack of information. Since the days of Moses, God has given the primary responsibility of teaching and training children to the parents:

These commandments that I give you today are to be upon your hearts. Impress them on your children. Talk about them when you sit at home and when you walk along the road, when you lie down and when you get up (Deut. 6:6-7).

Unfortunately, far too many parents abdicate their God-given responsibility of teaching morals and values to their kids by allowing the schools, TV or even their church to be their children's primary teacher. In fact, only 10 to 15 percent of adolescents tell us that they receive any kind of good, positive, healthy, value-centered sex education or drug education from home.[4] As a result, kids are making moral decisions based on too little information.

Today, there is a plethora of information on how to teach sex education. In 2010, on the very same week that the United States Government began to take away funding for abstinence-based programs, the *Washington Post* quoted a new pediatric study that indicates abstinence-based education is working in America. The public information coming out on sex education is a mixed message at best; however, there is one area on which all authorities tend to agree: the best positive, value-centered education comes from the home. I often tell parents that the more healthy information and dialog they have with their kids, the less promiscuous their kids will become.[5]

Proactive Parenting

There's no doubt about it: Being a kid today is much more difficult than it was when we were young. This means that producing a happy, healthy family takes more proactive work on our part than ever before. A proactive parent will look ahead at potential needs or problems and will take action to meet those needs or prevent those problems.

At the same time, we have fewer extended-family support systems in place and less time available to be proactive about providing healthy moral guidance and values for our family. And most of us parents didn't receive positive, healthy, value-centered education from home. Our parents may have tried, but their parents didn't do the job either, so most of us don't have many positive role models for providing the kind of training our children need.

Dave and Pam Hicks have been excellent examples to Cathy and me of what it means to proactively parent. They've reared four absolutely incredible daughters. One of their daughters, Carrie, worked as my assistant for seven years, so I have firsthand knowledge that they did a magnificent job! Years ago, Dave and Pam told Cathy and me one of their secrets to a healthy family life: Every six months while their children were growing up, Dave and Pam would leave home for the day or overnight when possible. They would talk about each child one at a time and discuss what they hoped to work on in that child's life for the next six months. They would write down their decisions and then review them during the next six-month period.

Cathy and I have chosen to follow their example and take time away to focus on our kids. We've made important decisions during these times: to take our youngest away for the mom-and-daughter sex talk an entire year earlier than the other two girls and to have more family fun days. Cathy and I both feel that our focused time away is a must for healthy parenting. When we become too busy to take time away, we're allowing circumstances and chance to take the place of proactive parenting.

Parents, it's time to bring morals and values education back home; it belongs there first and foremost. We must become students of the culture and take responsibility for equipping our children to develop sound biblical values and morals that will keep them from the dangerous influences of our culture. We don't have an easy job—we're bound to face some bumps, bruises and missed opportunities along the way—but let's take time to learn from the experts on the subject of morals and values. You can begin to teach family values to your children when they're young and continue as they move toward independence in the later teen and young-adult years.

Examining the Issues

This book is not meant to be the last word on morals and values, but I do want to take a look at several of the big issues, as well as suggest some practical steps for addressing those issues.

Sex and Sexuality

Your children deserve honest, open, blunt and unashamedly biblical answers in the area of sex and sexuality. Cathy and I like to go back to the list we make at our six-month meeting and then look for informal times and teachable moments to introduce the truths we hope to incorporate into our kids' lives.

Your interaction with your children must be age-appropriate and consistent. Books on child development and sex education will help you figure out what to talk about at what age. Don't be like the mother who was greeted by her seven-year-old son one day after school with, "Mom, what is sex?" The mother was shocked that the question came when he was still so young. *Where is my husband when I need him?* she thought.

Mom decided to face her fear and just go ahead and tell him everything. She pulled out a plate of cookies and a glass of milk and proceeded to give her son "the sex talk." She drew pictures. She gave proper names and functions of each intimate aspect of sex. Her son didn't say a word but listened intently—with his eyes as big as saucers—while finishing off all the cookies. Finally, after a very intense 45 minutes, the mother asked, "Son, do you have any questions?"

"Yeah, Mom, just one. I still don't know what I am supposed to write on my soccer form where it says 'Sex: Please circle M or F.'" He wasn't ready for the whole story; he just wanted to understand what he was supposed to write on the application!

Cathy and I created the following list of topics—relating to sex, dating and sexuality—that we want to talk about with our daughters. Keep in mind that sex education starts early and continues with age-appropriate disclosure throughout adolescence.

- Appropriate touch and inappropriate touch
- What the Bible says about sex and sexuality
- Definition of *puberty*
- Changes in hair and body, including body size and shape
- Menstrual periods
- Sexual organs
- Emotions

- Sexual attraction
- Infatuation versus real love
- Masturbation
- Pornography
- Sexual abuse, harassment and teasing
- Sexual intercourse
- Virginity
- Why wait?
- Pregnancy
- Dangers of premarital sexual relationships
- Partying
- The cultural influence of sex and sexuality
- Abstinence and purity
- How far is too far?
- Dating
- Homosexuality
- HIV/AIDS and other STDs

No matter the age of your child, it's important to teach your children what I like to call "the Purity Code." Obviously, we need to teach our children about sexuality from an age-appropriate developmental foundation. But even at an early age, we can begin to teach these words:

> **The Purity Code**
> In honor of God, my family and my future spouse, I commit my life to sexual purity. This commitment involves:
>
> - Honoring God with your body
> - Renewing your mind for good
> - Turning your eyes from worthless things
> - Guarding your heart above all else

When they are ages 3 to 5, we teach our children that God created boys and girls who will one day grow up to be mommies and daddies. We help them learn their basic anatomy, including their "private parts." Age 6 to 9 is the time of curiosity. We answer their questions (which may even begin at an earlier age) by teaching them about appropriate and inappropriate touch but also beginning to dialog about purity.

---

*Because of the early sexualizing of young
people by the culture, parents must be proactive
and intentional about building a healthy view of
God-honoring sexuality.*

Because of the early sexualizing of young people by the culture, parents must be proactive and intentional about building a healthy view of God-honoring sexuality. By the time this new generation of young people are ages 10 to 14, it is our responsibility as parents to communicate clearly about what sex is, what the Bible has to say about it and our expectations for their sexuality. Then, by the time a child is 14, anything goes when it comes to topics and dialog. You may feel awkward in conversation with your kids at first, but the alternative—your children learning what they want and need to know from a secular world that doesn't share your values—is, believe me, much more painful an option. (You can find more information on HomeWord's campaign for young people at HomeWord.com. Pure Foundations are excellent resources to help parents of children ages 3 and older live by the Purity Code.)

Media

The media is not neutral in our lives. In recent years, it has rapidly invaded almost every aspect of our world. In fact, during the past five years, there has been a huge increase in media use among young people. According to a report by the Kaiser Family Foundation, today's teens spend 7 hours, 38 minutes per day consuming media, which represents an increase of 1 hour, 17 minutes per day from 2004. This amounts to a full-time job! (It's even more when you take into account that the reported time consuming media per day is based on 7 days a week, not the standard 5-day workweek.) When multitasking is accounted for (consuming multiple sources of media at one time), today's youth consume 10 hours, 45 minutes of media content per day! That's an increase of about 2 hours, 15 minutes per day from 2004.[6] The retention level for the information received by reading this book (or any book) or listening to a speech is about 5 to 10 percent. However, the retention level for televised media is more than 25 percent.[7] This means that much of what your children put into their minds via TV, movies, video games and Internet is stored in the computer of their brain.

Parents must take a proactive approach to monitoring what enters their children's lives via media. We are fortunate because we have books, periodicals and the Web to help us learn more about the latest media influence. We can easily access reviews of movies and video games, the words of the popular songs kids are listening to, as well as the latest information on TV programming.

Television. The following tips to tame the tube have helped our family greatly but, in all honesty, have almost caused a few riots with a couple of the Burns teenagers! Despite that, they are a good guide to TV consumption for our home.

Tips to Tame the Tube

1. *Don't use the TV as a baby-sitter.* Usually, parents are extremely careful about choosing a baby-sitter and a day care for their children. Why are we not as careful about choosing the programs our children watch?

2. *Know what shows your kids are watching.* It is vitally important to know the content of every program your child watches. For younger children, videos are much easier to monitor. Ask the question, *Is the content in line with our moral guidelines?* If TV is not working to enhance your values, it may be working to oppose your values—and charging you a lot for it. Throw away the

remote, or at least save it only for Dad, when he *must* watch two football games at the same time!

3. *Don't put a TV in your child's bedroom.* A TV in your child's bedroom is a big no-no. You won't be able to monitor the content, and your kids will be drawn to their rooms at the expense of family interaction. A TV in the bedroom is a far too attractive temptation that easily interrupts such important matters as sleep, schoolwork, reading and interaction with others.

4. *Set limits on TV time.* What are your guidelines, rules and expectations for TV viewing? Can your children watch TV before school? How about before homework is finished? How many hours a day can the TV be on? Setting limits may be a challenge to your whole family, but when the limits are followed consistently, the results make them well worth it.

5. *Make an appointment with the TV.* It's a good idea to be proactive about your TV use and misuse. Many healthy families pull out the TV guide on a weekly basis and make TV appointments for the week, rather than having the tube on all the time as background noise. This monitors what shows your family is watching and how often, and it can make watching a TV program a family activity. Not too much butter on the popcorn though! Mom and Dad, why don't you make appointments with the TV, too? What children see, children do.

6. *Dialog with your children about TV shows.* All television is educational. The question is, *What does it teach?* Recently, I gave in to watching a movie on TV under the condition that afterward we would discuss it and react to it. Thankfully, the movie wasn't as gross as I thought it would be, and together we debriefed the

themes and content over frozen yogurt. We turned a mediocre movie into a first-rate learning experience.

7. *Make the DVR your friend.* If you can't watch the few good shows on TV because of your family's schedule, then record them and watch them as a family—the DVR can be your friend.

Internet. The World Wide Web is no doubt one of the most revolutionary developments in our generation, and it will only continue to influence and impact our lives in the future. My parents were one of the first families to get a small black-and-white television set in the little town they were from in Kansas. By the time I was born in California, the TV was a normal part of our family. Today, the Internet is a normal part of your children's education, recreation and communication with friends.

It's important to remember that each of these developments contributed to a vast array of changes that affected almost every aspect of life. However, of the five, the Internet will turn out to be the most important—the one that will change your children's lives in more ways than the other four. So fasten your seat belt and brace yourself for the ride of your life. This is the era of the Internet, and the Internet quite possibly will have more influence on your family than the television did in your parents' home.

Your children are growing up with one of the most incredible tools ever invented. Generally speaking, people 24 and older use the Internet as a tool, but people under 24 use it as a way of life.

Whether or not you are Web savvy today doesn't matter, but by tomorrow you had better be on your way to becoming an expert. Just because my 82-year-old dad doesn't trust an ATM doesn't mean that his children don't use them. When radio first came onto the scene, one famous pastor said, "This will never last." Like the radio, the World Wide Web is here to stay, and your children's lives will be changed forever because of it.

The Web is wonderful, but the Web is dangerous. Just like friends at school, it will either be a positive influence on your children or a negative one. So learn all you can about it and make it your friend. There has never been a time when the world had greater access to positive information and negative influences. Recent statistics show that 12 percent of websites are pornographic, amounting to 24,644,172 sites.[8] I'm glad that I'm not a 12-year-old boy anymore, tempted by the call of the darker side of the Web.

In the name of practicality, there are several steps you can take to help ensure that the Web is your friend:

A Guide to Safe Surfing

1. *Consider a quality Web filter for young children and young teens.* This is not the only answer, but it's a good start. (You can get many good ideas for Web filters by looking at the parent tip sheets at HomeWord.com.)

2. *Keep the computer with online access out of children's rooms or any backroom that is out of the way of people traffic.* I believe all computers in the home should come with family expectations of boundaries and accountability. Because so many teenagers have their own computers today, it complicates the issue of viewing privacy. However, I believe that even if your children have their own computer, there must be set rules and boundaries about use. My personal opinion is that it is just too tempting to allow your children to have Internet access on the computer in their bedroom. You may need to bring filters and other accountability software into the home to help manage this growing concern.

3. *Remind your child not to give out personal information over the Web without your permission.* With the advent of Facebook, MySpace and other online social networking opportunities, it is even more important for parents to help their kids understand the dangers of offering too much personal information. HomeWord is the nation's

largest provider of parenting seminars, and the number one question we receive from parents (regardless of the topic of the seminar) is, "How do I create a media-safe home?" This usually includes questions about Facebook and social networking. Many parents today tell their children that if they want to have Facebook, MySpace or any other social networking site, they must "friend" their parents. This doesn't mean that parents should ever make comments on their son's or daughter's Facebook page. While it is good for kids to know that their parents are their social networking "friend," a parent will always do better if he or she has a conversation about a concern rather than post it on a Facebook wall.

4. *Teach your kids that if someone interacts with them offensively online, they should report it to you right away.* Sexual abusers and predators lurk in some unique places. Don't hesitate to report any—and I mean *any*—questionable Internet activity to the local authorities. Didn't someone once say, "It's better to be safe than sorry"? As a parent, you're in the protection business.

Music. Another one of the greatest influences in your children's lives is the music they listen to. Don't buy the story that your children don't listen to the words. Music and musicians have a great deal of influence on our culture. MTV is not a music channel; it's part of youth culture. Learn what's influencing your kids during these very vulnerable years.

The music industry has rapidly moved from manufacturing CDs to placing songs for download on sites such as iTunes. The convenience is much greater and purchasing the music is sometimes cheaper, but parents must keep up with what kind of music is influencing their kids. Listening to your children's music downloads and, frankly, monitoring some of it is a necessity in the home today. Obviously, as your children move into the later teen years, they will have to make responsible decisions for themselves.

We try to listen to all the music on our kids' CDs and all their music downloads from iTunes and other sites. Sure, it takes a great deal of time, and we get to listen to some styles of music that aren't our favorite, but we must become students of the youth culture. We believe we have a God-given responsibility to review and, yes, even approve what words our children listen to in our home.[9]

I suggest that while your children still are young, you develop a music agreement and a media-viewing contract similar to the example given on the following page.

Drugs and Alcohol

When Steve Arterburn and I wrote the book *How to Talk to Your Kids About Drugs,* we were amazed at two statistics that kept popping up in our research. Ninety-two percent of all pastors said there was a problem with drugs and alcohol in their surrounding community, but only 13 percent thought there was a problem with drugs and alcohol in their churches. Incidentally, Christian parents believed the same. The second troubling statistic was that there was only about a 5 to 10 percent difference in the use and abuse of drugs and alcohol between kids who attended church and kids who didn't.[10]

There has never been a time when children were more susceptible to drug and alcohol abuse, and yet—without trying to offend you—most parents are either in denial or are ignorant of the issues of drug and alcohol abuse until it is too late. Parents of happy, healthy families study the threat of drug and alcohol abuse and teach their children about the dangers.

All parents should help their kids understand from a young age the usual progression of a young person's involvement with alcohol and drugs. A child or teen will begin to experiment with a gateway drug and then will continue along the road to dependence on hard-core drugs. Let me explain this process in more detail.

Beer and wine, the gateway drugs. Here's how they work: Kids begin their experimentation with beer and wine—that's usually where substance abuse begins. As I mentioned before, today the average first drink happens around age 12. The majority of kids will try

The Music Agreement

Hours music can be on in our home:

_____

Any groups or music not allowed in our home:

_____

Concerts the children may attend:

_____

Concerts the children may not attend:

_____

TV/Movie/Internet and Texting Contract

The average number of hours the TV can be on in our home per day is: _____.

The movie ratings that are available for each family member to view are: _____.

The TV programs that are not acceptable in our home are: _____.

A TV program that could be a fun family weekly date is: _____.

A movie that fits biblical standards that we can watch as a family is: _____.

A computer with Internet access cannot be in a bedroom without parent approval.

The average amount of time playing video and computer games per day is _____, understanding that homework and other responsibilities come first.

The agreed amount of texts per month is _____.

The boundary on texting during school hours is _____.

Child: _____ Date: _____

Parent: _____ Date: _____

alcohol before they graduate from high school. If kids do try beer and wine, they have a greater chance of moving through the gateway onto the road to substance abuse. Another step on this road is nicotine.

Nicotine. The tobacco industry has done a pitiful job of keeping future, underage addicts from experimenting. But is it really the tobacco industry's fault, or should the blame equally fall on us, parents who haven't taught our kids about the harmful effects of the very strong drug called nicotine? Did you know that it's actually easier to get off heroin than nicotine? The detoxification period of heroin is terrible, but after about five days, the drug has passed through the user's system. In contrast, some say it's nearly impossible to shake the habit of using nicotine because of its intensely addictive nature. The fact is that 81 percent of kids who smoke cigarettes will move farther through the gateway to experiment with marijuana, yet only 20 percent of the kids who do *not* smoke cigarettes will ever try marijuana.[11]

Eighty-one percent of kids who smoke cigarettes will move farther through the gateway to experiment with marijuana.

Harder alcohol. First of all, let's get something straight: Alcohol is a drug. It's a drug because it is mood- and mind-altering. It's also a poison; it's toxic. Most teenagers—and especially college students—know someone who has died or who became extremely sick from drinking too much alcohol.

All alcoholics have a high tolerance for alcohol and can consume a great amount without it affecting them like it does nonalcoholics. In fact, many budding alcoholics consume large quantities of alcohol; yet since they drink below their tolerance level, they are praised for being able to hold their liquor.

I know a 16-year-old young man who proudly told me he could drink five beers and not get drunk. He was surprised when

I answered, "I believe you, and in fact, I would rather have you as the designated driver than someone who is slushy drunk on two beers." But then I went for the jugular when I bluntly said, "You must be a budding alcoholic."

Surprised, he protested, "Maybe you didn't understand. I'm not even drunk after five beers."

I said, "I understand perfectly. Your body has a high tolerance for alcohol. The problem is, like all alcoholics, your body craves alcohol differently from that of nonalcoholics and will begin to break down. And unless you quit drinking, you will live a life very similar to your dad's." (He had already told me that he had little respect for his father, who was a drunk and who had left the family for his secretary. His father's alcoholism had messed up his own life and taken a toll on the whole family.)

Because our family has alcoholism throughout our family tree, we have had to teach our kids about this frightening disease; they—Christy Meredith Burns, Rebecca Joy Burns and Heidi Michelle Burns—are the three reasons I choose not to drink. I believe there is a biological predisposition toward alcoholism passed on from generation to generation. Since I have alcoholism on both sides of my family, I choose not to drink just in case it's in my system and in my daughters' genes. If they see Dad drink, they may justify their own drinking because of me. Because I'm aware of the issues, I am able to make conscious choices that will protect my children.

Marijuana. Marijuana, another step on this path to substance abuse, is similar to alcohol in that it's inexpensive, plentiful and intoxicating. When I graduated from Anaheim High School in 1971, we were told that marijuana wasn't harmful to our health. Hardly anyone is saying that today. We still don't know everything about this popular drug, but we do know that in many people it produces a sickness called amotivational syndrome, when one's brain is lazy and lethargic. Most of us have a friend or two who smoked just a bit too much pot, and although they function, they are just slo-o-o-o-w.

The other important factor for parents to know is that the marijuana in the 1970s is *not* the same as the marijuana kids are using today. Today's marijuana is 5 to 20 times stronger and is often laced with more dangerous drugs.

Heroin, LSD and cocaine. Then we move on to heroin, LSD and cocaine. Your children likely won't start their experimentation with these drugs, but as kids move through the gateway, they find it easier to violate their value systems and move to harder drugs. Each step past the gate brings people closer to hard-core drugs and brings more destruction.

Healthy parental drug education is an answer. The chances of young people abusing drugs lessen when parents proactively teach their kids and set a good example themselves. The first step in preventing your kids from abusing drugs and alcohol is self-examination. I know one father who tried to get help for his two sons for several years. On the day he admitted he had a problem with alcohol, his sons followed him into treatment.

Most likely, parents reading this book have made the decision to teach their children positive, healthy morals and values and to foster those values. Most parents are frightened by the amount of negative distractions and temptations facing today's kids. However, if our children are given proper education, a good example, positive faith and proactive parenting, they can make it through the maze of negative influences and develop positive morals and values that they will pass on to their own children.

DISCUSSION STARTERS

1. Who or what most influenced the development of your morals and values when you were a child?

_____

_____

_____

_____

2. What are your fears for your own children when you consider the moral decay prevalent in the world today?

_____

_____

_____

_____

_____

_____

3. What positive steps are you taking to protect your children and to help them fight the negative values of our day?

_____

_____

_____

_____

_____

4. What positive suggestions in this chapter were most helpful?

_____

_____

_____

_____

_____

5. How does the following passage relate to training our children to have biblical morals and values?

Train a child in the way he should go, and when he is old he will not turn from it (Prov. 22:6).

_____

_____

_____

_____

Alcoholism and Drug Use and Abuse Questionnaire for Parents

You may suspect that your child or teenager is having trouble with alcohol and other drugs, but short of smelling liquor on his breath or discovering pills in her pockets, how can you know for sure? While symptoms vary, there are some common tip-offs. Your answers to the following questions will help you determine if a problem exists:

1. Has your child's personality changed markedly? Does he or she change moods quickly, seem sullen, withdraw from the family, display sudden anger or depression, or spend hours alone in his or her room?

   Yes _____   No _____   Uncertain _____

2. Has your child lost interest in school, school activities or school athletics? Have his or her grades dropped at all?

   Yes _____   No _____   Uncertain _____

3. Has your child stopped spending time with old friends? Is he or she now spending time with kids whom you consider to be unhealthy influences? Is your child secretive or evasive about his or her friends, where they go and what they do?

   Yes _____   No _____   Uncertain _____

4. Are you missing money or other objects from around the house (money needed for alcohol and drugs), or have you noticed that your child has more money than you would expect (possibly from selling drugs)?

   Yes _____   No _____   Uncertain _____

5. Has your child been involved with the law in a situation involving drugs in any way? (You can be assured that if this has happened, there have been other times—probably many other times—when he or she has been drinking or using drugs and hasn't gotten caught.)

Yes _____   No _____   Uncertain _____

6. When you talk to your child about alcohol and drugs, does he or she get angry and defensive or refuse to discuss the topic at all? (People who are very defensive about alcohol and drugs are often hiding how much they use.)

Yes _____   No _____   Uncertain _____

7. Has your child become dishonest? Do you feel you're not getting straight answers about your child's whereabouts, activities or companions? (A young person may also lie about matters that seem unrelated to alcohol or drugs.)

Yes _____   No _____   Uncertain _____

8. Are there physical signs of alcohol or drug use? Have you smelled alcohol on your child's breath? Have you smelled the odor of marijuana on his or her clothing or in his or her room? (Slurred speech, unclear thinking or swaggering gait are also indicators. Bloodshot eyes, dilated pupils and imprecise eye movement may also be clues.)

Yes _____   No _____   Uncertain _____

9. Has your child lost interest in previously important hobbies, sports or other activities? Has your child lost motivation, enthusiasm and vitality?

Yes _____   No _____   Uncertain _____

10. Have you seen evidence of alcohol or drugs? Have you ever found a hidden bottle, beer cans left in the car, marijuana seeds, marijuana cigarettes, cigarette rolling papers, drug paraphernalia (pipes, roach clips, stash cans, etc.), capsules or tablets?

Yes _____   No _____   Uncertain _____

11. Has your child's relationship with you or other family members deteriorated? Does your child avoid family gatherings? Is your child less interested in siblings, or does he or she now verbally (or even physically) abuse younger brothers and sisters?

Yes _____   No _____   Uncertain _____

12. Has your child ever been caught with alcohol or drugs at school or school activities?

Yes _____   No _____   Uncertain _____

13. Has your child seemed sick, fatigued or grumpy (possibly hung over) in the morning after drug or alcohol use was possible the night before?

Yes _____   No _____   Uncertain _____

14. Have your child's grooming habits deteriorated? Does your child dress in a way that people in your community associate with drug or alcohol subculture? Does your child seem unusually interested in drug- or alcohol-related slogans, posters, music or clothes?

Yes _____   No _____   Uncertain _____

15. Has your child's physical appearance changed? Does he or she appear unhealthy, lethargic, more forgetful or have a shorter attention span than before?

Yes _____ No _____ Uncertain _____

How to Score the Test

This questionnaire is not scientific and is not meant to diagnose alcohol and drug problems. It is meant to alert parents when problems are likely. The questions are red-flag detectors, and your answers may show a need for further action. Keep in mind that "yes" answers to some of these questions may simply reflect normal adolescent behavior. "Yes" answers to questions directly relating to alcohol and drug use (5, 8, 10, 12) are, of course, cause for concern; they indicate that your child is using alcohol and/or drugs and that action should be taken.

In general, parents should look for an emerging pattern. A couple of "yes" or "uncertain" answers should alert parents to potential alcohol and drug use and should motivate them to monitor the child more closely, talk to knowledgeable sources and prepare to seek help.

If you answered yes to three or more questions, you probably need to seek help. Your child may be in the experimental stages or may already be heavily involved in alcohol and drugs. Remember, it is very, very difficult to handle this problem without the help of other experienced parents and/or professionals. Rarely is this a problem that passes with time; it may well be a life-or-death matter. Take action: Call a knowledgeable source such as a school counselor or an alcohol/drug counselor who deals with adolescents, your local council on alcoholism or another drug/alcohol agency and discuss this questionnaire.

4

Discipline with Consistency

We tried so hard to make things better for our kids that we made them worse. For my grandchildren, I'd like better.

I'd really like for them to know about hand-me-down clothes and home-made ice cream and leftover meatloaf sandwiches. I really would.

I hope you learn humility by being humiliated, and that you learn honesty by being cheated. I hope you learn to make your bed, mow the lawn and wash the car. And I really hope nobody gives you a brand-new car when you are sixteen.

It will be good if at least one time you can see puppies born and your old dog put to sleep.

I hope you get a black eye fighting for something you believe in.

I hope you have to share a bedroom with your younger brother. And it's all right if you have to draw a line down the middle of the room, but when he wants to crawl under the covers with you because he's scared, I hope you let him. When you want to see a movie and your little sister wants to tag along, I hope you'll let her.

I hope you have to walk uphill to school with your friends and that you live in a town where you can do it safely. On rainy days when you have to catch a ride, I hope you don't ask your "driver" to drop you two blocks away so you won't be seen riding with someone as uncool as your "mom."

If you want a slingshot, I hope your dad teaches you how to make one instead of buying one.

I hope you learn to dig in the dirt and read books.

When you learn to use computers, I hope you also learn how to add and subtract in your head.

I hope you get teased by your friends when you have your first crush on a girl, and when you talk back to your mother that you learn what Ivory soap tastes like.

May you skin your knee climbing a mountain, burn your hand on a stove and stick your tongue on a frozen flagpole. I sure hope you make time to sit on a porch with your grandma and go fishing with your uncle.

May you feel sorrow at a funeral and joy during the holidays.

I hope your mother punishes you when you throw a baseball through a neighbor's window and that she hugs you and kisses you at Christmas time when you give her a mold of your hand.

These things I wish for you—tough times and disappointments, hard work and happiness. To me, it's the only way to appreciate life.

—Lee Pitts, "These Things I Wish"[1]

• • •

When our oldest daughter, Christy, was 13 years old, we had a special meeting with her and told her we would buy her a car on her eighteenth birthday on the condition that she stayed drug-free and alcohol-free during her teenage years. We didn't promise a nice car, and at 13 she didn't really care about the kind of car. We promised that it would have four wheels and an engine that worked. About six months later, we added refraining from sexual promiscuity to the contract. I don't think Christy remembers that the sexual abstinence part was an add-on! I'm not even sure if Christy has been tempted much in the world of drugs and sex—she's a pretty exceptional kid. I do know that she tells her friends about our contract and that she wears a sexual-purity pledge ring as a covenant she made with God, her future spouse and her parents.

When I mention this particular contract idea on the radio show or in seminars, I get mixed reactions. Some parents don't like the idea at all, and others take their children out to dinner that night to do the same thing. Some look at it as bribing and others as brilliance. Only time will tell. The problem with developing contracts with our children is that each child responds to different kinds of boundaries in different ways. Cathy and I find that what works perfectly for Christy doesn't work with our other two daughters, Rebecca and Heidi. When Heidi was little, all we had to do was give her "the look" and she basically disciplined herself. Rebecca, who can have her father's stubborn streak, needed to be threatened with "a lifetime of grounding," and then it was very important that we stuck with our word.

Parent Training

Happy, healthy families have clearly expressed expectations with positive limits, boundaries and consistent discipline. And it isn't only the children who need to be taught. Parents are often the ones who need more help with discipline than their children. Let me tell you a story about that.

Our daughter Rebecca had been begging us for a dog for years. Cathy was willing, but I had put my foot down: "No dogs when the kids don't feed, clean or pay attention to the cats we already have." Now it was Christmastime, and Cathy found a beautiful golden retriever puppy that would be ready to arrive in a home on Christmas Day. I asked, "Who will groom the dog, feed the dog, scoop up after the dog, take the dog to the vet and walk the dog?"

"Of course the girls will" was Cathy's reply. Well, the dog was cute and I knew it would please Rebecca and all the girls, so in a weak moment I said yes. (Rarely is life easy for a male with all females in the house.)

Happy, healthy families have clearly expressed expectations with positive limits, boundaries and consistent discipline.

We picked up the dog late Christmas Eve with our friend Pam. What would we do with the dog until Christmas morning? I was already having second and third thoughts. Pam offered to stay at our house so I could sleep with the dog at hers. *Great,* I thought. It was Christmas Eve, and I was relegated to a vacant home with a puppy that stayed up most of the night and kept messing on Pam's rug—which I cleaned twice, at 3:20 A.M. and 4:45 A.M. When I arrived home bleary-eyed and exhausted by the events of the pre-dawn dog episodes, the girls saw the puppy and were ecstatic. We named him Hobie, after the line of surfboards.

All was well until we realized someone would have to clean the messes and train this puppy that had a passion for chewing shoes, curtains and wood tables. For some reason, I was elected to train the puppy to be just like our neighbor Bill's dog—the perfect dog.

I asked my neighbor, "Bill, how did you train Molly to be such an obedient dog?"

"Oh, it's simple," he replied. "Take Hobie to doggy obedience school and then work with him daily for at least 20 to 40 minutes." Oh, great! I'd been looking for a much quicker and easier answer.

The girls wished me luck as I picked Hobie up and literally carried him to his first day of puppy obedience school. When I got out of the car, I could see that Hobie was the rowdiest dog of the bunch. Furthermore, I wasn't sure if I was happy or embarrassed that the puppy trainer turned out to be a member of our church and began very enthusiastically to tell everyone about my work with youth and families. Just great. The "family expert" had the worst behaved dog in the entire group.

Our instructor said, "Today we will not work with your dogs." I was disappointed; I had hoped that by the end of the first class, Hobie would be fully trained. Our instructor continued, "Most of puppy training isn't really training the dog—that's the easiest part. Most of the training will be for you, the happy dog owners. Excellent dog training is at least two-thirds training the humans; the easiest part is working with the dogs." Then he shared the kicker. "I want to share with you four instructions right from the beginning that I actually learned from Jim, the man over there with the hyperactive golden retriever, when he and his wife taught a parenting class at our church." (I knew I was in trouble when all the other "happy dog owners" looked at me and I realized that my puppy was the only one that had tied up his owner's legs with the leash.) I just smiled and regretted both having taught that class and having brought home the puppy for Christmas.

He continued, "As Jim over there says, show lots of love and affection to your dog, discipline with consistency, set limits and boundaries, and express your expectations clearly to your dogs." Oh, great. I was having enough trouble following my own advice with my children, let alone this dog that had not stopped licking my shoes since the class began.

I'm happy to say, though, that Hobie passed the class. He is definitely my dog. And my instructor was right; I needed the training and obedience lessons more than the dog did. The skills Hobie and I learned really were similar to child-rearing skills. I needed to discipline with consistency in order for Hobie not to be an embarrassment to the entire neighborhood—especially to Molly next door.

Similar to dog owners, parents need more help with discipline than the ones they rear. Proper discipline is two-thirds parent training and one-third kid training. Disciplining our children consistently is the most difficult part of being parents. We establish the rules, we set the boundaries, and then we allow the rules to be broken by people who are one-third our age and have one-third our experience—usually when we want to be liked or because we're too tired to do what's right.

The Challenge of Consistent Discipline

Healthy parenting takes time, energy and work. As Focus on the Family founder James Dobson once wrote in his monthly newsletter:

> There is no assignment on earth that requires the array of skills and understanding needed by a mom in fulfilling her everyday duties.[2]

Dobson was absolutely right when he wrote this about mothers, and I'm sure he would agree that this also applies to fathers.

If you are having an easy time as a parent, something is definitely wrong. Quality parenting is the most important legacy you will leave in this world, but nobody said it would be easy. Your job is to help your children grow up to be responsible adults, not to be their best friend—that will come much later.

If you are married, you and your spouse need to make a combined effort to figure out your discipline strategy and then stick with it. If you are a single parent, you need the help and influence of others who can encourage you to be consistent with your discipline. For those who persevere, there is a great promise found in Proverbs 22:6:

> Train a child in the way he should go, and when he is old
> he will not turn from it.

Keep that promise in mind at all times when you are sticking to your strategy for discipline.

The purpose of discipline is to teach responsibility rather than to invoke obedience. There are many toxic ways to manipulate obedience, but if you use them, you will lose in the long run. Instead, your goal should be to move from control to influence. As children move through each stage of development—from dependence toward independence—they need different proportions and kinds of control, influence and discipline.

What children need most, though, are clearly defined expectations and consistency in the discipline they receive. The vast majority of kids in crisis that I meet tell me that they don't clearly understand their family's limits and expectations. Usually it's not the kids' fault but rather the parents' who are throwing out too many mixed messages.

One of the most difficult tasks for a parent is to be consistent. Many times we want our kids to like us so much that we compromise our discipline and send those mixed messages. Instead, we need to love our kids enough not to be their best friends. Part of disciplining with consistency is setting healthy boundaries for our kids and sticking to these boundaries. We need to care about whether they meet curfew, talk back, lie, do homework, steal, clean up after themselves and follow our family's moral code. We need to give consequences for actions that are not in line with the agreement. Your kids will love and respect you even more if you are consistent. Deep down they *don't want* you to be their best friend; and if you are doing a good job of discipline, you probably *can't be* their best friend.

One of the most difficult tasks for a parent is to be consistent. Many times we want our kids to like us so much that we compromise our discipline and send mixed messages.

One of my favorite questions to ask parents of teenagers in our HomeWord parent seminars is "How many of you could actually call your parents your best friends when you were a teenager?" Seldom does anyone raise a hand. Most of these parents say they didn't even *like* their parents during their toughest teen years—which might mean their parents were doing a good job. Being a parent who disciplines with consistency is no easy road and is not for the faint of heart; but rest assured that if you do bring boundaries and God-principled discipline to your home, your kids will one day thank you for it—just probably not today or tomorrow!

Choices and Consequences

Most of life involves choices and consequences, so good parenting involves teaching our children the cause-and-effect relationship between the two. If you make wise choices, usually the consequences are positive. If you make poor choices, then negative consequences will ultimately follow. Proverbs 26:27 expresses this idea: "If a man digs a pit, he will fall into it; if a man rolls a stone, it will roll back on him." Not only will consequences follow your children's choices when they are young, but consequences will also follow their choices all of their lives.

Some parents are a bit too rigid with choices and consequences, but by far, significantly more of us struggle to be consistent. We have opinions about movies, music, friendships, talking back, curfew, lying and hundreds of other issues; but because of our own humanity and an incredible need to be liked, we often miss the mark and are inconsistent when it comes to teaching our children that there are consequences for almost every choice they make. As parents, we need to make it our goal to consistently discipline our children in the areas of choices and consequences. There are several ways to do so.

Involve Your Children in Consequential Decision Making

If you were to ask your child, "If you choose to disobey me and turn on the TV when you know you are not allowed to have it on, what would be a good consequence for your behavior?" what would you expect her response to be?

You probably wouldn't expect her to say, "Actually, Mom, I understand exactly what you're saying. If I turn on the TV, you'll have the right to take away TV privileges from me for an entire weekend. If I do it a second time, then I'm grounded from the TV for a week. A third time really needs to have a major consequence, like no soccer for two weeks. And, Mom, thanks for looking out for me and my future. I will be a much more responsible adult and marriage partner because of these consequences." Right! When it comes to creating consequences, don't expect your child to have a positive response; however, when the consequences to various actions have been discussed ahead of time and your child has helped decide the consequences, she will tend to more readily accept the results of her choices.

One day when our daughter Rebecca was 14 years old, she went to the park five houses away from our home without telling us. Obviously, this was not an offense worthy of capital punishment. However, she knew the Burnses' rules on going someplace without telling us. The only way we knew she was at the park was that her older sister had seen her talking with some of her friends as she drove past the park. As much as I didn't want to embarrass Rebecca, a deal is a deal and a consequence is a consequence. I drove to the park to pick her up. She balked a little but got in the car. The first words out of her mouth were, "I'm busted! I should have asked you or Mom."

"You're right, Rebecca," I answered. "The crazy thing is I would have been glad to allow you to go to the park or invite your friends to our house."

She asked, "What's my consequence?"

"You tell me, Rebecca."

"No phone or computer for the day?"

"Right!"

"Can I go back to the park, Dad?"

"No, you lost that privilege for the day."

I wish I could tell you disciplining always goes that smoothly, but you never can predict what any of our reactions will be. Rebecca could have been frustrated with me; but because she had been a part of discussing and creating the consequences in the first place, she knew she had already signed off on the consequence by not telling us where she was going. She also knew that the consequences get stiffer with a repeated offense, and by the third time she would lose the privilege of a special school event.

Remember: Your job is not to try to be your children's best friend; rather, it is to train them to be responsible adults.

Make Sure the Consequences Fit the Crime

Our children should expect minor consequences for minor infractions and major consequences for major infractions. Some parents tend to panic when their children begin to rebel just a bit, but we should be consistent and not overreact to our children's moving toward independence. If they are a few minutes late on curfew or didn't clean up their rooms, it doesn't mean that they need to be placed on restriction for the rest of their lives.

When we pass out consequences that don't fit the crime, we usually renege on the consequence anyway, and that produces inconsistent discipline and more potential problems. At the same time, if our children continue to be disobedient over a period of time and we don't offer appropriate consequences, we are not teaching them the lifelong lessons they need to learn.

Discipline Calmly
Neither Cathy nor I can find any Italian blood in our family trees
(although we sure like pizza!), but our house is anything but
quiet most of the time. Here's our goal: We don't discipline our
kids when we are angry. Otherwise, we'll usually say or do something we don't mean.

---

*Leave the phrase "you will never" out of
your discipline vocabulary. When we are angry or
full of empty threats, we are often not very consistent
with our consequences and discipline.*

Leave the phrase "you will never" out of your discipline vocabulary. Don't tell your kids that they are out of the school play
unless you really, really mean it. Threats don't work. When we are
angry or full of empty threats, we are often not very consistent
with our consequences and discipline. Sending mixed messages
to our kids usually gets in the way of the lesson we are trying to
teach them.

Express Your Expectations Clearly
Your expectations must be clearly stated, and the consequences
must make sense to your child. If we constantly offer unrealistic
expectations, we are most likely not doing an effective job in the
discipline department. Be absolutely clear, ask your children to
tell you what they understand, and if you must, write down your
expectations.

Saturday morning is workday around the Burns house, but
for most of our 20 years of child rearing, it has been more of a
hassle than a joy. We finally decided to take a different approach:
We write down on a paper each of the agreed-upon chores for
the morning. If our kids want to do anything—from watching
TV to spending time with their friends—they must wait until all
their chores are finished before making their requests. Should

they choose not to do chores, then they are making the decision not to spend time doing fun weekend activities. If they want to sit in their pajamas all day and delay their chores, that's up to them—as long as their choices don't get in the way of other family activities. "Freedom comes after chores" is our motto. This plan has worked for us, but we have found that we must put it on paper and let the kids know we mean business when it comes to consequences.

The Family Contract

Perhaps one of the most effective consequence and discipline tools is what many call the "family contract." Basically, the family contract involves discussing and putting on paper the expectations and agreements about certain behaviors or issues in the family. The family contract helps kids discipline themselves.

You will find that the clearer you are with the issues and consequences, the easier it is to manage a family contract. Don't go overboard and make their entire lives a family contract, or you will lose the powerful results of the contract. Focus on behaviors and their attitudes will follow. Keep your contract simple; and whenever possible, have your children help create the family contract, because they will support what they create.

I've included here two sample contracts, so you can see what I'm talking about.

I know one dad whose son was caught ditching class. After the son had ditched for the second time, the dad sat with his son in class for two weeks. His son never ditched again! This is a bit harsh for some families, but clear and expressed expectations of behavior are a must.

A family can use contracts or understandings similar to those just described, but regardless of the method, children do better when they have a crystal-clear understanding of what is expected and the consequences of not following through. A chart of family rules and a discipline checklist are two other tools that some families use to help their kids and themselves work on constancy.

Simple Family Contract

Issue: Sloppy habits at the dinner table
Expectation: Good table manners
Positive Consequences:
- A general feeling of happiness and contentment
- After a week of good table manners, a special treat or dessert
- After a month, an art project or special weekend outing to celebrate the victory

Negative Consequences:
- No TV for the evening
- Go to bed a half-hour early
- No phone privilege for the weekend

More Severe Family Contract

Issue: A failing grade (you have already tried other methods to bring up the grade)
Expectations: Raising the grade to a C with zero-tolerance for not turning in homework
Action steps:
- Teachers sign weekly progress report.
- Teachers sign daily homework assignments.
- You will have a daily homework check-in with Mom after school and with Dad at the end of the evening.
- You will have a weekly check-in time with Dad about school, grades and attitude.
- You may choose to be in the school play. If you do not choose to do the agreed-upon schoolwork, then you are choosing to take yourself out of the play. (This is called reality discipline.)

Positive Consequences:
- Teachers will not have to sign the daily homework sheets.
- After a C grade, we will not need to have a weekly progress report.
- If the grade is an A or B, then we celebrate with a new outfit or special event.

Negative Consequences:
- We have a meeting with the school counselors and teachers.
- We suspend phone or weekend privileges.
- If nothing else works, then we consider homeschooling or changing schools.

Family Rules

Each rule should include the following:

The rule: _____

The reason for the rule: _____

Negative consequences: _____

Positive consequences: _____

Tip: If you decide to use a list of family rules, narrow it down to 10 or fewer so that everyone can easily remember them without carrying around a legal textbook!

Ultimate Discipline Checklist

Here is a tool for you to help you think through your response to your child's behavior:

1. The behavior I want changed is: _____.
2. How might I be feeding, or enabling, the problem behavior?
3. Will I give the child a choice or is the behavior a must?
4. My clearly stated rule is: _____.
5. The consequences are: _____.
6. My follow-through will be: _____.
7. Will I be consistent, no matter what it takes?

How to Keep Your Child's Spirit Open

All families will have conflict, and there are times when we, as parents, will have to confront, discipline and not be the most popular people in our children's lives. However, when we discipline, we do not want to close the spirit of our child toward us. When children have a closed spirit, they usually avoid communicating with us. They may withdraw, be contrary and refuse to show affection, and they may say very mean and hurtful words. Children with an open spirit, on the other hand, feel reassured of their parents' love. They are open to criticism, even though they don't like it, and they bounce back quite quickly from negative conversations. Children with a spirit that is open to their parents are willing to communicate and to show affection in an age-appropriate way, and they are much more open to building healthy relationships with their parents.

The simple saying, "Rules without relationship lead to rebellion," is so very true when it comes to keeping a child's spirit open in the midst of discipline. A friend of mine with many problems as an adult once told me, "I was scared to death of my dad. He ruled with his fist and the belt. He forced obedience in the house when he was there, but every one of us moved out as quickly as we could and had problems dealing with intimacy and relationships partly because of the way Dad handled us as children."

When it comes to discipline, our kids need us always to show respect, even in the midst of tension. We can disagree with our children and still be able to communicate with gentleness and respect. All relationships have conflict, but a relationship between two people whose spirits are open to each other can take the conflict in stride and work through it in love.

Do Not Nag

Nagging definitely is not the best way to keep a child's spirit open. Sometimes we simply need to have the self-control to keep our mouths shut until we find a better and more effective way to share our concerns with our children or spouse. I've never had a kid tell me that he or she greatly benefited from Mom's or Dad's nagging. Nagging is a lazy habit many of us learned from our own parents. However, there is a better way to discipline and a better way to communicate.

Choose Your Battles Wisely

The parent who becomes defensive toward his or her family is the parent who is trying to manage too many battles on too many fronts. Does your child's room need to be as perfect as your room? If that is your battle, then win the fight; but if it isn't worth fighting for, then compromise.

Cathy is much more of a neatnik than any of the rest of us. When we were first married, we had to find a satisfactory settlement on clean rooms. Over the years, Cathy has trained me to pick up my clothes, put the dishes away and not leave stuff everywhere. Unfortunately, she now has three daughters who, thank God, look more like their mom but clean more like their dad. The compromise isn't always easy for Cathy. We've negotiated that we expect clean rooms on Tuesdays and Saturdays. That's two more days than our girls would choose and five fewer days than Cathy would like. But we've chosen compromise and negotiation because it's just not an important-enough battle. When parents fight too many battles, their children may close their spirits to their parents.

Listening is the language of love, and empathy is more valuable than you would ever imagine in keeping the spirits of your children from closing when you must discipline.

Show Empathy

Many parents need improvement in the areas of eye contact, tone of voice and body language. Often our body language tells our children more than our words about our availability. Listening is the language of love, and empathy is more valuable than you would ever imagine in keeping their spirits from closing when you must discipline. Our kids have feelings; we have to show respect for their feelings as well as for their privacy. Discern in which areas of their lives it is not critical for you to intervene, and then stay out of their business in those areas.

Do Not Discipline in Anger

When a child's spirit is broken and closing, it is often because they feel attacked by their parents' anger. You can attack the behavior, but you should not attack the person. You need to choose your words carefully, because words can either build up or destroy your children.

One family I talked to was having major problems between the mom and the teenage daughter. Significant problems can be normal, but this daughter's spirit was almost totally closed to her mother. The young girl was definitely a spitfire—she might be called the poster child of the strong-willed child. I could see why there would be conflict, but I couldn't understand why the daughter's spirit was so closed to her mother, who seemed to be a very nice woman. Then the daughter gave me some insight. She told me that when her mother got angry with her, she would hear two constant themes: "I hate you" and "You are the reason that your father and I got a divorce." Even if, in her heart of hearts, the mother had moments of believing those abusive words, she should have kept them to herself. The teenager felt rejected, hated, blamed and attacked. Most of the time the mother was a good mom with a loving attitude. However, those powerful, destructive words were keeping the spirit of her daughter closed toward her. Anger doesn't get kids to obey. Action, love and consistency do.

To keep from disciplining when you're angry, you may need to do what one father did. He was pushing a stroller through a city park. The baby was screaming at the top of his lungs. It was a summer day, and the park was filled with people who were watching. As the young, embarrassed father passed by, he was heard saying in a forced calm voice, "Take it easy, Malcolm. Now, now, just relax. No reason to get excited. Just calm down and everything will be all right. Come on, Malcolm, just settle down and trust the Lord."

An older woman who was watching stopped the man and said, "My, what a nice baby. Did you say his name was Malcolm?"

To which the frustrated father replied, "No, ma'am. His name is Joshua. I'm Malcolm."

Remember that all relationships have conflict, but a relationship between two people whose spirits are open to each other can take the conflict in stride and work through it in love.

Disciplining with consistency is one of the answers to having a happy, healthy family. What's amazing about discipline is that it takes an incredible amount of self-discipline on our part to be consistent and to clearly express our expectations. Just about the time we resolve to make the right discipline decisions, our children manipulate us into moving away from our resolve. Or we act on our natural desire to protect our children from difficulty and disappointment. When we fail—and we will—we must pick ourselves up and again be consistent. Our kids will thank us 20 years from now.

DISCUSSION STARTERS

1. How would you describe the type of discipline you received growing up?

_____

_____

_____

_____

_____

_____

2. In what ways is your approach to discipline similar to your parents' and in what ways is it different?

_____

_____

_____

_____

_____

3. Have you ever used a contract for your child? If so, how did it work?

_____

_____

_____

_____

4. What elements in your life make it difficult, at times, to keep your child's spirit open?

_____

_____

_____

_____

_____

_____

5. How do the following proverbs relate to disciplining with consistency?

Train a child in the way he should go, and when he is old he will not turn from it (Prov. 22:6).

If a man digs a pit, he will fall into it; if a man rolls a stone, it will roll back on him (Prov. 26:27).

_____

_____

_____

_____

_____

_____

5

Ruthlessly Eliminate Stress

I feel absolutely dry and overextended. I'm a people-pleaser by nature, and I feel like my busyness is letting others down. My overload is affecting my intimacy with Cathy, and I don't feel as close to my daughters right now. I'm busy being with people, but I'm feeling lonely. Many a day I do not look forward to work because I know that I will have to deal with the urgent and not the most important. I'm tired and fatigued. I want to work out and eat better, but I keep putting off what is healthy for what is easy. I'm craving friendships, and I'm too busy to even attempt to get together with some of the guys. God is getting some of my attention, but not what I dreamed it would be by this time in my life. I used to be a lot more fun.

—From my journal

• • •

Living at Breakneck Speed

Perhaps the greatest problem in parenting is the breathless pace at which we live our lives. I love the story of the first grader who wondered why her father brought home a briefcase full of work every evening. Her mother explained, "Daddy has so much to do that he can't finish it all at the office."

"Well, then," asked the child innocently, "why don't they put him in a slower group?" As the pace of life gets more and more unhealthy, perhaps it is time to join the slower group.

The Definition of Crisis–Mode Living

Are you experiencing what some like to call the "overload syndrome"? It's what happens when you do not have what Richard Swenson calls *margin*. Margin is the space that exists between our load and our limits. Margin is the space between vitality and exhaustion. It is our breathing room, our reserves, our leeway.[1] Healthy families have figured out how to live with balance and margin, but unfortunately, such families are few and far between. As a friend of mine says, "We work hard, we play hard and we crash hard."

Margin is the space between vitality and exhaustion. It is our breathing room, our reserves, our leeway. Healthy families have figured out how to live with balance and margin.

It was the great philosopher Vince Lombardi of the Green Bay Packers who told his teams over and over again, "Fatigue makes cowards of us all." When I'm fatigued and living in crisis mode, I am a lousy husband to Cathy, a poor excuse for a father to my children and a mediocre president of HomeWord. I have a sign in my office that reads, "If the devil can't make you bad, he'll make you busy." Most families are so busy doing good things that they miss doing what is most important.

You probably already know if the overload syndrome is plaguing your life and your family, but if you're not sure, ask yourself these questions:

1. Have you stopped enjoying life because you are too busy?
2. Have you stopped developing new relationships?
3. Are you exhausted most of the time?
4. Do you and your spouse have a regular date night?
5. Does your family have an enjoyable dinner together on a regular basis?
6. Do you get enough sleep?
7. Do you take a restful day off?
8. Do you have regularly scheduled family times together?
9. Do you have credit problems or a large debt load?
10. Are your children showing signs of stress?

If you struggle with many of these questions, then you are among the majority of families who are living in crisis mode. Let me be blunt: You are flirting with disaster. That disaster will be either yours, your spouse's or your children's. Crisis-mode living paralyzes families.

Crisis-mode living is when you spend almost every waking moment trying to figure out how to keep all your plates spinning in the air. In crisis mode, you keep running faster and faster, from project to project, deadline to deadline, quota to quota, meeting to meeting, folding laundry to carpool to . . . you get the picture. Your life's RPM is in the red, and you believe you have no other option but to keep on running, faster and faster. You fear that if you stop, the plates will crash. And frankly, some of the plates *will* crash if you stop; but if you don't stop soon, the results likely will be much more damaging to the physical, emotional and spiritual health of you and your family.

The Damage of Crisis–Mode Living

When we live in crisis mode for too long, we begin to skim relationally. Virtually all our relationships are damaged by hurry. Many families are relationally starved because of overcommitment and fatigue. If you are married, your bond with your spouse, which was once strong and intimate, becomes weak and distant. Sometimes our children lie wounded, run over by high-speed intentions. Our children have watched more videos than is healthy, simply because we don't have the strength to spend time with them. When we skim relationally, friendships slip away. We quit our support groups and miss our family outings. We find our relationships fading. Friendships that were deep and meaningful are now shallow. Casual relationships hardly even exist. Pretty soon no one has access to our souls.

Crisis mode even causes us to skim spiritually. What was once a burning desire to serve God has become relegated to a few prayers and a dull faith—the kind of faith that we said we would never have. In Eugene Peterson's beautiful translation of the Bible, *THE MESSAGE*, he paraphrases the apostle Paul, who was talking about people like you and me:

They were so absorbed in their "God projects" that they didn't notice God right in front of them, like a huge rock in the middle of the road. And so they stumbled into him and went sprawling (Rom. 9:32).

Crisis-mode living also causes us to skim emotionally. When we are too busy, we tend to ignore the emotional side of our lives. We may find our anger flares up more than it used to, and we don't take the time to figure out why. Our patience with our children wears thin. We quit paying attention to feelings like hurt, sadness or guilt. We become mechanical soldiers marching through our days—just doing what's necessary while we stuff our feelings deeper and deeper inside. We're emotionally depleted, but we keep on pushing. The results aren't pretty!

When we live in crisis mode, we also neglect dealing with the problems and issues in our lives. One of my experiences in the spa—the most relaxing spot in the world for me—illustrates this truth all too well.

One night, we were going to have a family meeting in the hot tub—my daughters know I'm a pushover when I'm sitting in the spa. I love to sit there; when I turn up the heat and turn on the jets, my burdens seem to disappear. On this night, as in most times my family soaks in the spa together, I had gotten in a good 10 minutes before my wife and my daughters did—why it takes men so much less time than women to change clothes and put on a swimsuit, I have no idea. Actually, I didn't mind, because those jets felt so good against my back and my pressures were fading away.

The jets stopped, and as I soaked in the hot, still water, I noticed that our spa was filthy. We had recently experienced a windstorm, and the spa had collected leaves, dirt and just plain old grime. I had been sitting in filth, but because the jets were churning up all the dirt, I hadn't even noticed. As I heard the girls and Cathy coming, I realized I had two options: I could either take the time to get out of the spa and clean all the grease and grime, or I could quickly turn the jets back on so that my family would not realize they were sitting in dirty water. So what did I do? Need you ask? I quickly turned those jets back on, and we had our family meeting in our polluted spa. My wife and daughters never knew!

Unfortunately, too many of us live our lives like that. We seldom take the time to deal with our life issues and problems; instead, we just keep on pushing, hoping that the marriage will get better or that the subtle, negative signs we see in our kids will disappear by themselves. Well, they won't. For too many years, I have heard myself say to Cathy, "As soon as we get past this season in our lives, then it will slow down." But as seasons turn into years, crisis mode continues for many of us, giving us more reasons to skim relationally, emotionally and spiritually. A solid, healthy family builds margin into their lives and deals with their problems before they become catastrophes.

Creating Margin

How does a family overcome the overload syndrome and create margin? No easy answers here, just some important—but sometimes difficult—choices. Healthy families are made, not born. So let's roll up our sleeves and get to work. The sacrifice is real, but the payoff is well worth it.

Give Time to Your Family

One of the most famous business writers of this century recently wrote that to succeed in business you have to give up a great deal. In fact, he said that few people can be both successful in their business lives and involved with their children's activities, such as by coaching a son's Little League team. When I first read those words, I was angry. Who did he think he was to give some dads who are already doing a poor job as fathers the idea that to be successful they have to sacrifice even more time with their children? Why can't you be successful at both parenting and business? Believe me, I know several men and women who are successful at both.

However, I think the business author is actually right. The successful businessperson almost always sacrifices family time to make it to the top. So, as a person who wants to be successful in my career and who also wants to have healthy family relationships, I've had to learn—sometimes the hard way—this principle: *The unbalanced life will not be kind to the areas we neglect.*

Go ahead and coach your son's Little League team, but take a few more years to climb the corporate ladder. For goodness' sake, don't neglect your family.

If your schedule is constantly out of control because you are trying to do too much, you will reap the results: an unbalanced family life and an unbalanced work life.

Since I believe in the power of being there for my kids, I spend less time in the office, which means fewer things get done there. It means turning down speaking engagements that would help my career. It means rearranging a flight to be at my daughter's homecoming game and flying the red-eye to speak the next day, tired. In order to practice the power of being there with your kids and to live a more balanced life, you must give up some of your other interests. Yes, you will probably lose some profit in the short run; but if you neglect your family and your marriage for the sake of your business, your long-term effectiveness as a parent will be at risk. If you focus on your family as a priority, then you often simply won't be as successful in your business. See, I told you it wouldn't always be easy! But if your schedule is constantly out of control because you are trying to do too much, you will reap the results: an unbalanced family life *and* an unbalanced work life.

I would nominate Tom Yankoff for Dad of the Year. Successful in business? You bet. A terrific and involved dad? No doubt. But Tom wasn't always a nominee for Dad of the Year. He was the typical competitive businessman who showed his love for his family by working long hours. The money started coming in, and the square footage in his new house increased dramatically over his old one. He drove nice cars, his family took nice vacations and his kids attended the prestigious private school in their area. They looked like the all-American, rich, successful, healthy, churchgoing family.

Tom was too busy to think much about the occasional gnawing feeling that all was not right at home. He knew that his marriage to Dina was stale, but he really didn't want to work on it. She was encouraging him to attend counseling with her, but that only ticked him off. *After all, we're not crazy,* he'd reason. *Sure, my anger flares and I'm not always there for my two sons, even when I'm with them; but I have a lot to do and a lot is on my mind.*

His two boys were making him a bit nervous—they were straying a bit from their family's morals and values—but Tom figured that boys will be boys. Many times he came home to conflict that he was too tired to deal with, so he either settled the problem with his anger or hid behind more work or sleep or sometimes church involvement.

Tom wasn't a bad guy. He went to church. He voted! But he skimmed relationally with his family. In his mind he reasoned, *What successful person doesn't?* Tom and his wife came from classic dysfunctional families, and he questioned, *So what is normal, anyway?*

Tom thought that a good vacation might solve their family problems. He was proud of himself that he had taken the time to plan a very special family ski trip. He would reconnect and have a great time with his boys and Dina. His office could surely function without him for four days!

On the first day of skiing, he and his older son, Trevor, jumped on the ski lift to go straight to the top of the mountain. He looked over at Trevor, and it was as if he had been hit over the head. As he stared at his son, whom he deeply loved, he realized that he didn't know the names of his son's friends or if his son liked a special girl. He couldn't name any of his teachers. He didn't know his favorite color. The more Tom thought about what he didn't know about his son, the worse the situation looked in his mind. By the time they slid off the chair lift, Tom was in tears. Trevor had no idea what was going on. Was his dad having a heart attack or a nervous breakdown? After three hours of talking and praying and crying—the emotional release of his life—Tom skied down the hill and quit his job!

Pretty dramatic decision, huh? Tom knew he needed to do more than just correct a few out-of-balance habits. He had to give up his mistress: his job. Tom signed on as the boys' football booster club president. He went to counseling with Dina for their marriage. He joined a men's support and accountability group at his church. He found time to reconnect with his family. Of course he had to find another job, but this time he went into it with his eyes open and decided that with God's help he would build a support system to keep his family priorities in balance.

Tom has led the way for his family to be part of the transitional generation of people who will live a healthier life than the previous generation, and today, both of his children would definitely nominate him for Dad of the Year. Have you ever met a person who said, "I wish my dad [or mom] had spent more time at the office when I was growing up"? I haven't.

Do Less and Rest

I like the story of the man whose life had been notoriously cluttered, busy and confused. After he died, the epitaph etched on his tombstone read "Organized at last."

When it comes to adding more activities to our already overcrowded lifestyles, there is a word in the English language that far too many families don't use enough—the word "no." Should we add one more event to our already crowded schedule? No! Lindsey is in soccer, church youth group, drama club and tennis, but can she still squeeze in piano lessons? No, she can't. Even though she wants to add another activity, is it really worth it? Far too many kids are growing up with too much stress because they are just too busy doing good things.

Two words of advice for the busy schedule are *eliminate* and *concentrate*. As crazy as this may seem, I want to give you permission to cut back and do less. More is not always better. Doesn't it feel good when you finally get around to cleaning out the closet? Do you really miss the stuff you threw away? I doubt it. If you slow your pace down a bit, you'll feel better and so will your family. Cathy has a favorite saying that hits me right where it counts—in my heart: "Jim, we already have a Messiah who has done wonderfully for more than two thousand years. Don't replace Him!"

Cutting back involves resting and relaxing. Rest must be a non-negotiable in your schedule and in your family's schedule. Rest heals, soothes and gives perspective. For the generation who invented the 24/7/365 mentality, it is important to remember that even God rested on the seventh day of creation: "In six days the LORD made the heavens and the earth, and on the seventh day He rested and *was refreshed*" (Exod. 31:17, *NKJV*, emphasis added). Refreshment is such a great concept.

When Cathy and I celebrated our twenty-fifth wedding anniversary, we took a 10-day do-nothing-and-plan-nothing trip up to Canada's beautiful British Columbia coastline. The tranquil setting, the long walks, the lingered-over meals and the loving, tender touch were exactly what we needed to sweep out some of the cobwebs of our relationship and return to the deep love that we had felt 25 years earlier. We rested, and we were refreshed. We came home wondering why we had waited so long to have those kinds of experiences.

When was the last time you were refreshed? When was the last time you proactively replenished your family relationship? It was probably longer ago than you wish, and you are most likely looking for the next time to be as soon as possible. Sometimes people will stop me and say, "You must be really busy." Yes, I am busy, but they are implying that busyness means success. How unfortunate that some of the busiest people we know are some of the unhappiest—people who rarely take time to rest and relax.

Here's a fairly simple question: Do you take at least one 24-hour day off each week from your work? This includes homemakers! Of course the kids still need to be fed, but do you ever rest? According to authorities, North Americans are busier than ever and rest less than they did at any other time in our history. If you are not taking at least a 24-hour rest from your work, I believe you are pressing toward burnout—if you are not already there. Most likely, if you do not have times of quality rest, then your primary relationships are disheveled. (Your primary relationships are with your spouse, children, special friends, God and even yourself.) Rest won't restore a broken marriage or put a poor relationship with your child back together, but it sure will get you started in the right direction.

Rest won't restore a broken marriage or put a poor relationship with your child back together, but it sure will get you started in the right direction.

Sometimes I work too hard and take life too seriously. Last week I noticed flowers in my backyard in full bloom—I had missed the process of blooming. Life is too short. Sometimes we need to sit back and enjoy God's gifts to us. It's time for another generation to be reminded of these reflections of a wise man toward the end of his life:

> If I had my life to live over again, I'd try to make more mistakes next time. I would relax. I would limber up. I would be sillier than I have been this trip. I know of very few things I would take seriously. I would take more trips. I would climb more mountains, swim more rivers, and watch more sunsets. I would do more walking and looking; I would eat more ice cream and fewer beans. I would have more actual troubles and fewer imaginary ones.
>
> You see, I am one of those people who live prophylactically and sensibly and sanely, hour after hour, day after day. Oh, I've had my moments, and if I had it to do over again, I'd have more of them. In fact, I'd try to have nothing else. Just moments, one after another, instead of living so many years ahead each day. I have been one of those people who never go anywhere without a thermometer, a hot water bottle, a gargle, a raincoat, aspirin, and a parachute. If I had it to do over again, I would go places, do things, and travel lighter than I have.
>
> If I had my life to live over, I would start barefooted earlier in the spring and stay that way later in the fall. I would play more. I would ride on more merry-go-rounds. I'd pick more daisies.[2]

Fight for Solitude

Do you ever take time to be silent? I am by no means an expert on living life as a monk, but great health and peace can be found in solitude. As you read the New Testament, you will often see that the strength that enabled Jesus to be with energy-draining people was found in His quiet moments. Often right before a very busy time of ministry He would go away to a lonely place and pray (see Mark 1:35; Luke 6:12).

The spiritual discipline of solitude has been all but lost in our twenty-first-century, hurried lifestyle. However, healthy families ruthlessly eliminate as much hurry and clutter from their lives as possible and pursue moments of solitude. Spiritually speaking, solitude is being with God and God alone. Is there space for solitude in your life? In solitude you will hear the whisper of God's voice saying, "You are My beloved, the apple of My eye. You are doing a wonderful job parenting those kids. I treasure you, I forgive you and I believe in you. You are My child, and we are in this parenting thing together."

If you never find time for solitude, you will hear another voice shouting at you, "You aren't good enough; you are a failure as a parent and spouse. You aren't spiritual enough or pretty enough or rich enough. Your life is a waste." But in solitude we hear the voice of God reassuring us that He loves us and is proud of us. If you keep that thought in mind and find moments of solitude and rest, then you can deal with an enormous amount of failure as well as an enormous amount of success because your identity is based on the unfailing love of God.

In solitude, I ask myself three questions that help me find perspective:

1. Do I like the human being I am becoming?
2. Is the work of God I'm attempting to do with vocation and family destroying the work of God in me?
3. How often does my family receive only my emotional scraps?

Many times I do not like the answers I give to these questions in the quiet moments of my soul. Busyness paralyzes our souls, but solitude and rest bring us hope.

Stressproofing Our Kids

Adult stress-related diseases have never been worse, and authorities tell us that adult stress-related disease has its roots in childhood. It's a simple fact that stressed-out parents almost inevitably pass their stress along to their children. The only good stress is stress that is short-lived.

Medical, psychological and spiritual authorities agree that stress is affecting our children in negative ways. Our stressed-out children today are in poor shape physically, mentally and spiritually. Dr. Archibald Hart, one of the world's leading authorities on stress, has noted the severity of the stress children experience:

> Today's children are faced with double jeopardy. They face a world that is more stressful than ever. In addition, they are forced to depend less and less on their traditional source of support—their families.[3]

We parents must do something to ease stress in our children's lives. The good news is that once we understand where the stress in our homes is coming from and how it affects our children, we are well on the road to preventing more stress damage in their lives.

Gordon and Vicki were living the busy life of a pastor and spouse in a highly successful church. Their home was filled with love, but because of the family's extremely busy schedule, the children didn't have a regular bedtime. Both children kept getting sick and would often miss school, which affected their grades and self-image.

Finally, Vicki had a long talk with the family pediatrician. This gentleman was active in their church and knew the lifestyle of this busy family. He sat Vicki down in his office and said, "I have a hunch why things are physically deteriorating with your children and why both of them are struggling with school. Vicki, you and Gordon are too busy, and the kids do not have a regular enough schedule or specific bedtime routine. Your kids are great kids, but they are sleep deprived."

Vicki didn't expect this answer; she and Gordon had considered getting the kids tested for ADD and other learning disorders. Gordon and Vicki took the doctor's advice, and both sacrificed their work schedules to give their children more of a routine and more sleep. Within three months, both of their children had raised their grades from Ds to Bs, and the entire atmosphere of their home had dramatically improved.

Gordon and Vicki are my heroes because they recognized that there was a problem, sought advice and then made adjustments to their lives to guard their children from experiencing more stress than they could handle. It takes courage and sacrifice to make bold decisions, but that is exactly what some families must do to stressproof their home.

To determine whether or not your child is overstressed, take the excellent "Is My Child Overstressed?" test, created by Dr. Hart.[4]

Is My Child Overstressed?

Child's name _____

Carefully review your child's behavior and complaints for the previous two or three weeks and rate the following questions using this scale:

0 = My child infrequently feels or experiences this.
1 = My child sometimes (perhaps once a month) experiences this.
2 = My child experiences this often (between once a month and once a week).
3 = My child experiences this frequently (more than once a week).

____ 1. My child complains of headaches, backaches or general muscle pains or stiffness.
____ 2. My child reports stomach pains, digestive problems, cramps or diarrhea.

___ 3. My child has cold hands or feet, sweaty palms or increased perspiration.

___ 4. My child has a shaky voice, trembles and shakes, displays nervous tics or grinds and clenches his or her teeth.

___ 5. My child gets sores in the mouth, skin rashes or low-grade infections like the flu.

___ 6. My child reports irregular heartbeats, skipped beats, thumping in the chest or a racing heart.

___ 7. My child is restless or unstable and feels blue, or low.

___ 8. My child is angry and defiant and wants to break things.

___ 9. My child has crying spells, and I have difficulty stopping them.

___ 10. My child overeats, especially sweet things.

___ 11. My child seems to have difficulty in concentrating on homework assignments.

___ 12. My child reacts intensely (with angry shouting) whenever he or she is frustrated.

___ 13. My child complains of a lot of pain in many places on the body.

___ 14. My child seems anxious, fidgety and restless, and he or she tends to worry a lot.

___ 15. My child has little energy and has difficulty getting started on a project.

Total: _____

Test Interpretation

0-5 Your child is remarkably low in stress or handles stressful situations extremely well.

6-12 Your child is showing minor signs of stress. While it is nothing to be concerned about, some attention to stress control may be warranted.

13-20 Your child is beginning to show signs of moderate stress. Some attention should be given to how your child copes with stress.

21–30 Your child is showing significant signs of stress. You should give urgent attention to helping him or her reduce stress levels.

Over 30 Your child appears to be experiencing very high stress levels. You should do everything possible to eliminate stressful situations until your child can learn to cope. You may want to consider getting professional help.

Note: You may want to go over the test items that have been answered with a rating of 2 or above to better understand the signs of stress in your child's life. See where you can provide relief and help your child build more resistance to stress. If you feel that your child's problems—no matter what his or her score on this test—are beyond your ability to handle, then seek professional help immediately.

After you have taken the test, you'll want to make sure that you remember the common physical and emotional symptoms of stress in your child. Sometimes it's difficult to discern what is normal child or adolescent behavior and what has its roots in stress-related disease. If you see symptoms in your own children or are confused about them, then I would strongly suggest that you seek the help of a counselor or pastor. The Bible is clear: "Where there is no counsel, the people fall; but in the multitude of counselors there is safety" (Prov. 11:14, *NKJV*).

The key physical symptoms to look for are headaches, dizziness or lightheadedness, heartburn, stomach problems, generalized body pain, grinding of teeth, skin eruptions, frequent infections or minor illnesses, sleeplessness and loss of appetite—to name a few. The emotional symptoms are sometimes more difficult to determine, but they include anxiety and panic reactions, depression, general lethargy, outbursts of anger and irritability.

If you see stress as a problem in your home, then it's time to reexamine your family's lifestyle in order to help your children succeed. Start with the basics: getting adequate sleep, keeping physically fit, providing plenty of room in your schedule for relaxation and making sure that you don't overcommit. If you try these basic—but not necessarily easy—steps and things are still not improving, then it's time to get a professional involved before more problems arise that will carry on into your child's adulthood.

DISCUSSION STARTERS

1. How would you characterize your stress?

   ❑ We are extremely overcommitted and fatigued—in need of margin.
   ❑ We're managing our stress fairly well.
   ❑ Stress is not a problem in our home.

2. "The unbalanced life will not be kind to the areas we neglect." What concerns do you and your family have right now?

   _____
   _____
   _____
   _____
   _____

3. What difficult decision might you have to make to ruthlessly eliminate stress for you and your family?

   _____
   _____
   _____
   _____
   _____

4. If you took the stress test, how did your children fare?

_____

_____

_____

_____

_____

_____

5. How does the following Scripture challenge or give hope to you and your family?

Even youths grow tired and weary, and young men stumble and fall; but those who hope in the LORD will renew their strength. They will soar on wings like eagles; they will run and not grow weary, they will walk and not be faint (Isa. 40:30-31).

_____

_____

_____

_____

_____

_____

6

Communication Is the Key

My boyhood goal had always been to play on the La Palma Little League all-star team. It was now a reality. We were playing West Anaheim, and I was pitching. What should have been a dream come true became a nightmare.

It started in the first inning: The lead-off hitter walked; the second guy hit a shot to right center field for a double; then I walked the third batter. With the bases loaded, I hung a curve ball, and the clean-up hitter cleaned up! He put that curve ball over the fence for a grand slam. Ouch!

I felt humiliated.

After only four batters, the coach moved me to shortstop, where I made three errors in the next five innings. I also struck out twice. Needless to say, it wasn't a good day.

But now it was the last inning, and I had a chance to redeem myself. We were tied up, 6-6, and the bases were loaded as I walked up to bat. Until this day, I had the best batting average in the league. Despite my earlier strike-outs, everyone seemed confident that I could win the game for La Palma.

First pitch: I watched it go right over the plate—strike one. Second pitch caught the corner—strike two. I was feeling the tension. I stepped out of the batter's box and looked at my dad. He gave me the thumbs-up sign. The third pitch came straight down the middle of the plate. I watched it go by—strike three.

I almost single-handedly lost the game! The other team emerged as the champions.

I had never been more miserable in my life. I cried like a baby. I didn't want to talk to anyone, especially my dad. All my life, he'd played catch with me, hit me grounders and threw batting practice for me. He had always been there to instruct and encourage me. Now I'd let him down. I knew he'd be disappointed. I couldn't face him.

After we unenthusiastically congratulated the other team, our coach told us it had been a great year. He said we should be proud. Yeah, right!

I couldn't put it off any longer. I had to face my dad. I slowly gathered my glove, bat and jacket and then looked up. There he was, running toward me. I knew I'd failed him. I was sure he was going to say something like, "You should never watch three strikes go by when the bases are loaded."

Instead he rushed over to me, gave me a big bear hug and literally picked me up. Instead of anger, he had tears in his eyes and said, "Jimmy, I'm so proud of you."

That night we ate a couple of cheeseburgers and drowned our sorrows in chocolate milk shakes. He told me a story about a time he'd failed miserably in the most important game of the season. We laughed and cried together. My dad never was very mushy, but when I saw the tears in his eyes, I knew he loved me and that everything would be okay.

● ● ●

That day my dad communicated unconditional love and acceptance to me. A few years ago, my then-82-year-old father came over to our house. We were sitting outside enjoying the warm California sunshine when I asked, "Dad, do you remember the Little League all-star game when I was 12 years old?"

"Oh, sure, you struck out looking at the last pitch!" He smiled.

Thirty-four years after that game, I felt tears well up in my eyes. "Dad, thanks for being so understanding back then. Even after I struck out, you told me you loved me and that you were proud of me."

Now tears welled up in his eyes. "I am still proud of you."

"Thanks, Dad," I said, giving him a hug.

Later Cathy asked me, "What were you two talking about out there? It looked like you were crying."

"Oh, we were just remembering a Little League all-star game when I struck out with the bases loaded," I told her. I think Cathy's reply was something like, "Men are so strange!" That may be true, but my dad had communicated love to me.

When it comes down to it, the healthier the family, the more effective the communication. One of the primary problems of any dysfunctional family is lack of quality communication. Communication is behavior. It's an action word, and it must never stop. Communication is the means, not only the goal; it is more about the interaction than the outcome.

You can win the battle and still lose the war in communication. When communication fails in a family, it is not usually because of the content but rather the relationship. I always smile when I ask couples in premarital counseling, "How well do you communicate?" No one has ever said, "Horribly!" They usually respond that they can tell each other everything or that they can talk for hours. One year after a couple is married, I always invite them back for a conversation. Invariably, they say, "Our number one problem is communication."

When communication fails in a family, it is not usually because of the content but rather the relationship.

Communication is about *perception*. Oftentimes, though parents try to communicate with their teenagers, the teens do not believe that their parents are communicating with them at all. In fact, many times in our HomeWord family seminars, I ask parents and their kids if they believe they are communicating. Almost invariably, the parents say yes and the kids say no.

Most of us didn't grow up with very good role models for communication, and if we don't learn helpful tools, we will pass on poor communication skills to our children. Likely no one would disagree that healthy communication takes focus, discipline and hard work. It involves at least two elements: *content* and *relationship*. The previous generation may be guilty of focusing more on the content of communication than on the relationship. However, when communication fails, as I mentioned, usually the problem is not the content; it is usually the relationship.

Do you remember the father in one of the most famous musicals ever made into a movie, *The Sound of Music*? Captain Von Trapp loves his children, but when he arrives home from his busy travels, he runs the house like the military. His communication style is "captain to private." He has control for the moment. He gets his children's obedience, but Maria, the nanny who later becomes his wife, passionately begs Von Trapp to prioritize relationship over content. His relationship with his children changes and he evolves into a loving parent; it makes all the difference in the world.

Parents like Von Trapp, who practice the captain-to-private type of communication, are employing shame-based parenting. As we discussed in chapter 2, shame-based parenting brings rules without relationship, which causes rebellion. In healthy communication between parent and child, by contrast, there is positive give-and-take. The child knows who is boss, but the relationship is based on affection, warmth and encouragement.

What's difficult about communication is that if our parents used shame-based parenting, we will lean in the same direction. If our parents tried the high-volume solution, we will find ourselves doing the same when we are desperate. If sarcasm was a part of our family growing up, then odds are that we will need to work harder not to use this communication-killer with our spouse and children. There are several other communication-killers, which include verbal overkill, classic put-downs, argument shift, silent treatment and "the preacher." I actually think I have tried all of these at one time or another and discovered that they just don't work in the long run.

Now let's look at some communication strategies that work.

Use the Languages of Love

When you use a language of love, you and your family members are able to communicate effectively—you are able to understand what each other is saying.

Listening—A Language of Love

One of the greatest gifts you can offer your children is the gift of listening. When you listen, you show that they have great value to you. My problem is that when my children are wrong or have a poor attitude, I want to immediately correct them instead of honor them by simply listening. A young girl recently said to me, "I've quit sharing and telling my mom anything because I know I will just get a lecture. Mom wants a relationship with me, but she is not willing to sometimes just listen to me and leave it at that." Good observation.

Active listening doesn't come easily for most parents. Yet taking the time to really pay attention, show empathy and listen to our children may be the most important part of long-lasting and healthy communication between parents and children. Recently, when discussing the need to listen more effectively, one mother said, "I try to listen. I really do. But I guess I rarely follow through. Too often I break into the middle of a story that I perceive isn't that important or I already know where my child is going with it and give my opinion. Life is so complicated and busy that I wonder if my listening while multitasking ever bothers my children." Of course it does.

I think it is time to put down the newspaper or let the dishes wait or record the ball game and find ways to communicate by simply listening to our children talk. Effective listening involves a genuine desire to listen to your child, a willingness to accept your child's feelings and emotions whether your child is right or wrong, the ability to accept not always being right, a nonjudgmental attitude, eye contact, being attentive through body language, expressing to your child that you feel honored to have the kind of relationship in which they share their heart with you and a willingness not only to listen but also to keep in touch and be supportive.

Five Other Love Languages

I have often teased that between the number of Gary Chapman's books that I have purchased to give away and the number of times I have suggested that someone buy his marriage and parenting resources, I have probably helped purchase his family's home. His material on the five languages of love is a part of my life and my communication vocabulary. In his book *The Five Love Languages,*

Chapman explains that we all have emotional and love tanks, and he describes excellent communication as keeping other people's tanks full. We help keep them full by using the love languages that are most meaningful to them. When we help keep our spouse's and our family's tanks full, we will communicate well and have healthy relationships with them. If we gamble with our family and spouse by keeping those tanks near empty, communication is much more difficult.

The five love languages Chapman identifies are *words of affirmation, quality time, receiving gifts, acts of service* and *physical touch*. He says that most of us have a primary love language and perhaps a strong secondary love language, although all of them can be important for good communication and healthy relationships.[1]

Let's look at the five ways to express love and to communicate, and then let's try to figure out which primary love language will fill your children's tanks, as well as your spouse's.

1. *Words of affirmation.* In training our children, we tend to criticize failure. If overdone, this can create devastating consequences in adult life. Determine to praise your child for every right thing done during the next week. A minimum of two compliments a day is a good goal.

2. *Quality time.* Get down to your child's level. Discover his or her interests and learn as much about him or her as possible. Be totally present, giving your child undivided attention. Make time each day to give your child (or each of your children) at least a few minutes of quality time. Make it a priority.

3. *Receiving gifts.* Gifts, if overdone, can become meaningless and teach a child a false set of values. But periodic gifts, thoughtfully chosen and given with affirming statements such as, "I love you, so I got a special gift for you," can help meet a child's need for love. The next time you buy or make your child a gift, express your

love verbally as you present the gift. (You may also express your love as you refuse to give your child something you think is inappropriate: "I love you, so I will not buy you a rattlesnake for a pet.")

4. *Acts of service*. Though you constantly perform acts of service for your children, the next time you complete a task especially meaningful to your child make sure that you say it means you love him or her. Pick a task that is not especially appealing to you but that is very important to your child. Learn a new skill in the academic or mechanical area to become a more well-rounded parent.

5. *Physical touch*. Hugging, kissing and appropriate touching are very important for a child's emotional tank. Consider the age, temperament, love language, etc., of each child and determine a unique approach in this area. When your child gets older, you will need to be sensitive, but you should still maintain a regular habit of touching for affirmation.[2]

As you discover your child's primary love language, focus on using it regularly—but do not neglect the other four. The others will be even more meaningful once you are speaking your child's primary language. Now ask yourself, *Which of these communication love languages meets my primary need? How about the primary needs of my spouse and children?* Practice filling the love tank of each family member by communicating in his or her love language.

Communicate Honesty and Integrity

You don't have to be perfect, but kids do not want to follow the leadership of a hypocrite either. The parent who tries to come across as perfect is making a big mistake. Believe it or not, apologies improve communication. Let your children know you're human. Admit your mistakes and take the perfection pressure off. Admitting your mistakes clears the channels for real communication and removes barriers that may be in the making. Admitting mistakes promotes sharing and oftentimes creates warmth and understanding.

Admitting failures also curbs unrestrained idealism. What I mean is that if your children go too long observing unreal parents who act as if they have no problems or flaws, the eventual shock of watching parents fail can end up being destructive. When you are honest about your imperfections with your children, you open up the way for a more mature type of problem solving. If your kids feel valued enough that you would share a struggle or a hurt, they will most often respond maturely. One caution is not to get in the habit of dumping all your problems or marriage issues on your children. They are your kids, not your counselors.

---

*If your children go too long is observing
unreal parents who act as if they have no problems
or flaws, the eventaul shock of watching parents
fail can end up being destructive.*

Several years ago, I took a sabbatical from my work so I could finish writing my Ph.D. dissertation. My entire family picked up and moved to Hawaii for three months. I know you feel sorry for us, but somebody had to do it! Cathy is an educator by training and I made it through high school, so we decided to homeschool our children during our time away. Things were going pretty well until I realized I could get a Ph.D. more easily than I could help Christy with sixth-grade math. My definition of "hell" is a place where they do math word problems, and that is exactly what Christy was studying during our homeschooling experience in Hawaii.

One morning, there was a great deal of tension in our home. The younger girls wanted to ditch school and go to the beach. They were grumpy. Cathy was reacting to their grumpiness while Christy and I were struggling through the worst math word problem in the universe. I was anxious to get to my dissertation, and Christy was anxious to get away from me. In the middle of the word problem, she snapped at me, and I went crazy. I'm embarrassed to admit it, but the veins in my neck exploded with anger. I verbally slayed Christy right there in our living room, with Cathy, Rebecca and Heidi looking on in disbelief. Usually I'm the guy who is even-keeled, but not this time. "How dare you?" "Don't you understand?" "How selfish can you get?" and "Furthermore . . ." were all things I said in that angry moment. Then I sent her to her room.

The house grew eerily quiet. My two younger girls had looks of fear, and Cathy's look was somewhere between disgust and disbelief that I would go crazy over a math word problem and Christy's bad attitude. I decided it was time to get out of the house; I slammed the door for added effect. Then I went to the water's edge and sat down.

After about 15 minutes of blaming everyone but myself (including my own sixth-grade math teacher), I came to my senses and humbly walked back into the house. Cathy was working with the other girls, and Christy was in her room. Cathy glanced up for a moment, saw my contrite expression and pointed to Christy's room. I gave a gentle knock—no answer. I opened the door. She was lying on her bed with tears in her big green eyes. I came alongside her bed, got down to her level and said, "Christy, I am so sorry. I hope you will forgive me. That was all about me and not about you." With tears still in her eyes, she put her arms around me and said, "I forgive you, Daddy, and I'm sorry, too."

A few years later, Christy was being "hormonal and emotional" with her mother. The rest of the family stopped what each was doing to listen in on Christy and her mom having a big disagreement. Christy was being rude, so I stepped in and very calmly told her to go to her room and cool down. I told her that I would be up in a few minutes and we would talk. She sputtered all the way up the stairs to her bedroom and slammed the door. To me it was just nice to have some peace and quiet as the rest of the family went back to homework, chores and fixing dinner.

Almost an hour later, as dinner was about to be served, Cathy asked me how my talk with Christy had gone. Being the great father that I am, I had to admit to Cathy that I had enjoyed the peace so much that I had actually forgotten to go talk with her.

I hurried upstairs and tapped on her door. In a very quiet voice, she told me to come in. She was lying on her bed with tears in her eyes. She stood up, and before I could say a word, she blurted out, "Daddy, I am so sorry! That was all about me and not about you guys. Will you forgive me?"

"Of course I will, Christy. I love you and I'm proud of you. In fact, I think I've heard pretty much those same words before from someone else. Do you remember?"

"Of course I do, Daddy. And I love you and I'm proud of you, too."

The moral of the story is, be an authentic parent who isn't afraid to apologize when you see the need. Proverbs 10:9 says, "The man of integrity walks securely," and the children of the man or woman of integrity will walk securely as well. (The other moral of the story is, don't do sixth-grade math word problems if it's not your specialty!)

Invest Time in Communication

I disagree with the parenting specialists who say that if you can't give your kids quantity time, then give them quality time. I think your kids deserve both. I find that my finest discussions with my own children come during the quantity times, not the so-called quality times. I'll be driving one of the kids someplace and—bingo!— the conversation leads to a very important topic. I just slow the car down and get in as much time as possible. As we discussed in chapter 1, proactive communication comes naturally when we spend a great deal of time with our children. It's easier to get that time when our children are younger, but it is never too late.

I find that my best conversations happen when food is involved. Each week, I try to connect with each of my girls over a quick meal or treat. One morning, I took Rebecca for a bagel breakfast and then dropped her off at school. Then I turned around and took Christy to the same bagel shop before dropping her off—good conversations and a few more calories for me.

A friend of mine gives his kids a nightly backrub. He wanders into their rooms right about bedtime and begins massaging their shoulders. He tells me it is amazing how they begin to open up about their days when he starts rubbing their backs. Another friend writes her children letters. Often, a letter is better expressed and better remembered than verbal words; many of us express ourselves far more effectively when we write than when we speak. Sure, it takes time to find a card and write the note, but the dividend is communication lines that stay wide open.

Allow Conflict to Be a Path to Deeper Communication

Does this kind of conflict ever happen in your home?

> "Dad, Heather just called. Can I go over to her house to watch a movie?"
>
> "Rebecca, ask your mom." (In other words, *I'm too distracted*.)
>
> "Mom, Dad said I should check in with you before I go over to Heather's house to watch a movie."
>
> "Your dad said it was all right?"
>
> *Pause.* "He didn't seem to mind."
>
> "Have you finished your chores? Did your dad check your homework?"
>
> *Distraction from the question.* "Dad said it was fine with him if it was okay with you. Heather could use some company because she had a really bad day."
>
> "Well, all right, but be home by 8:30."
>
> *Twenty minutes go by.*
>
> "Jim, why on earth did you let Rebecca go to Heather's house? She didn't even start her chores, her room is a mess and it doesn't look like she finished her homework."

"Cathy, I didn't say she could go. I told her to check in with you."

"Jim, you could have asked about her chores, looked in her room or even quit watching that game and either helped me with some of the work around here or at least checked on Rebecca's schoolwork."

Jim is now angry. After all, he has spent a difficult day writing books on how to have healthy families. "Hey, Miss Perfect, why didn't you check Rebecca's homework and chores, and if you didn't work so hard, maybe everybody around here would be a bit happier."

"You're just like your father!"

"Well, you're becoming just like your mom!"

Conflict can either be a path to communication blockage and unloving behavior, or it can be a path to deeper communication, greater understanding and loving behavior. When there is a conflict, the natural inclination for parents and their children is to become defensive and closed in order to protect themselves. The defensive, closed path of conflict involves avoiding personal responsibility for feelings, behavior and consequences. It immediately leads to shame-based parenting, when we try to control through guilt, manipulation and, sometimes, fear.

Another negative way to deal with conflict is to avoid it—to keep the peace at all costs. Some parents, as their children get older, deal with conflict by becoming overly permissive and withdrawing emotionally from the situation. The result of taking the closed path of conflict—whether through guilt, defensiveness, control or over-permissiveness—is that the child's self-image is eroded and he develops feelings of tension, frustration, anxiety and anger. In the short term, it may be easier to handle conflict by being defensive or closed in order to protect our own fragile self-image; but if we stay defensive and closed, we will wind up with more power struggles and burdens. However, there is a better way.

The better way to handle conflict is to be nondefensive and open to learning about each other, with the intent to deepen intimacy. With this in mind, we must assume responsibility for our own feelings, behaviors and consequences. Working through the conflict takes greater emotional involvement, but it is the loving way to care for yourself as well as your child.

Most of us didn't learn to handle conflict in a healthy manner, so this process of exploration makes us more vulnerable to being affected in a negative manner by our children's concerns. If you are open during conflict, you are willing to experience transitory pain or fear to get to the truth about the problem. It means being a bit less judgmental, and it involves exploring defense mechanisms, values, responsibility and feelings of fear, pain, inadequacy and vulnerability.

One time, Christy and Rebecca were on an airplane with me. They were both wearing earphones and listening to music. This lack of communication is a pet peeve of mine. However, I had allowed them to bring the music players on the plane. I tried to get their attention by snapping my fingers at them. Christy calmly said, "You're snapping your fingers at me like I'm a dog."

I growled back, "If you weren't wearing those earphones, we could communicate."

She replied, "All you have to do is tell me, Dad. Plus, snapping is demeaning."

I wanted to get defensive. Instead I simply said, "You're right. I'll try to be more sensitive next time." Our conflict was resolved, and life moved on.

The positive side to being open during conflict is that your children will sense a greater feeling of security. They will be able to take on more personal responsibility and be less defensive in conflict because their self-image is intact. When you choose this path, I believe you will see an almost immediate improvement in family unity, security and peace in the home.

Of course, dealing with conflict in an open manner does not mean that we as parents do not have the last word or don't need to discipline our children with consistency. The Bible's instruction, "He who spares the rod hates his son, but he who loves him is careful to discipline him" (Prov. 13:24), perfectly illustrates that as parents we are called to guide and lead our children toward a healthy lifestyle. Teaching them a healthy way to handle conflict is one of the most important ways to accomplish this. It will bring your family more and more intimacy.

Whether it be a lack of conflict resolution or listening skills or an overcommitment that keeps you from communicating, your children will follow your example of communication. Parents must take the lead in this area of family relationships. If you don't, your children will develop some of the same poor communication habits you may have inherited from your own parents. Now is the time to drop your defenses and put away your pride. Now is the time to develop intimacy in your family relationships by becoming a more effective communicator. There is always room for improvement and, believe me, you set the pace for your children. If you find yourself needing help in the area of communication, there are excellent books, seminars and counselors to assist you. Don't delay. Communication is the key to a happy, healthy, solid family.

DISCUSSION STARTERS

1. In which areas of communication and intimacy does your family struggle in its relationships?

   _____

   _____

   _____

   _____

2. Who in your life is a good role model for communicating and why?

   _____

   _____

   _____

   _____

3. Can you identify the love language of your spouse (if you are married) and each of your children?

_____

_____

_____

_____

_____

_____

4. How would you rate your family's ability to handle conflict and communicate during conflict?

1	2	3	4	5

needs attention   so-so   great

5. How can you use the advice of the following verse in a practical way with your family?

Therefore encourage one another and build each other up, just as in fact you are doing (1 Thess. 5:11).

_____

_____

_____

_____

_____

_____

_____

Rate Your Family IQ
(Intimacy Quotient)

How close is your family? Dolores Curran, author of *Traits of a Healthy Family*, evaluates 15 traits necessary to make healthy families.[3] The following questionnaire is adapted from her research. Our family has used it to help us evaluate our family intimacy quotient as well as our level of communication.

How to Take This Test

Rate the intimacy quotient of your family by responding to the questions. Award yourself points for each answer as follows:

1 point: We're definitely not there yet.
2 points: This is sometimes true of our family.
3 points: This is usually true of our family.

_____ 1. In our marriage, my spouse and I share power equally, complementing each other's strengths and weaknesses.

_____ 2. At the dinner table, our family shares more than food. We also share ideas, feelings, disappointments and dreams.

_____ 3. If there is a conflict between a family tradition and an outside responsibility, the family tradition usually wins.

_____ 4. As parents, we allow our children freedom to make decisions in certain areas and expect them to accept the consequences of those decisions.

_____ 5. Our family shares together in at least one leisure activity a week.

_____ 6. As parents, we are aware of our children's facial expressions, body language and physical gestures and from these pick up clues that lead us to ask appropriate questions and initiate honest discussion.

_____ 7. The basic, underlying mood of our family is hopeful and forward looking; we have our sources of stress, but we consider them temporary and manageable.

____ 8. When we are alone together, my spouse and I are vulnerable to each other and risk exposure of our deepest feelings.

____ 9. We allow our children to make choices among various activities outside the family, but we do not allow these activities to interfere routinely with our leisure time together.

____ 10. We have different rules for children of different ages.

____ 11. We know what we believe, and we find strength in our faith.

____ 12. We have a vision as a family and seek to be involved in something bigger than the quality of our relationships.

____ 13. We have our share of problems, but we usually can see the positive in every situation, no matter how bad.

____ 14. No matter how busy we are, our entire family eats a meal together at least once each day.

____ 15. My spouse and I agree on what is right and wrong.

____ 16. We make an effort to gather regularly with those in our extended family.

____ 17. We refuse to remove obstacles from our children's lives that will potentially foster their growth and responsibility.

____ 18. As parents, we occasionally spend time alone with each of our children.

____ 19. We keep our work commitments under control and do not allow them to routinely crowd out family.

____ 20. Although we go through rough periods, we stick together and try to make things right.

____ 21. In our family, we make each other feel important by supporting each other in our failures as well as in our successes.

____ 22. As parents, we allow our children to be exposed to situations in which they can gradually earn more trust or rebuild trustworthiness.

____ 23. When conflicts arise, we give everyone a chance to speak and work at negotiating solutions before the conflicts become volatile.

____ 24. Different personality styles and preferences are accepted within our family life.

____ 25. Our definition of success is not based on promotions, possessions or power but on the quality of our service to others.

____ 26. We laugh at ourselves and with each other, and we use humor to defuse potentially stressful situations.

____ 27. As adults, we provide for our kids a value system out of which certain rules and accepted behaviors arise.

____ 28. We present opportunities in our home for our children to prove their capabilities.

____ 29. The underlying religious attitude of our family is one of moving closer to a shared core of spirituality.

____ 30. We expect and allow our children to change as they get older. We respect their fads, friends, confidences, privacy and time—their right to be alone and their right to be different—as long as these things are not destructive.

Total: _____

Now add up your total points. If your total score is:

1-30   Your family has the potential to become an intimate family if you are willing to apply energy and determination to the process.

31-60 Your family has a strong foundation upon which to build further intimacy.

61-90 You are maintaining strong momentum in the direction of intimacy.

Play Is Necessary for a Close-Knit Family

Seventeen years is a long time to know someone, and Ron's parents thought they knew him. What had happened during the previous summer, though, Ron's parents had no idea. All they knew was that when school began, their "normal," straight-A son had become a "punker." Black was the only color he would wear—a black Metallica T-shirt, black pants, black motorcycle boots—and with his earring-adorned ears (seven earrings total), shaved head, and obsession with heavy metal music, the seventeen-year-old Ron showed very little resemblance to the sixteen-year-old version. Mom and Dad were worried. Home had become a war zone. Each day when they came home from work they'd have to storm downstairs to Ron's locked bedroom, where the music was so loud the walls were shaking. They would bang on the door and loudly ask Ron to turn down the music.

After six months of escalating tension, Ron's parents decided to get counseling before they lost their child. Many issues came to the surface and the process went on for many months, but one of the solutions the counselor suggested sounded so bizarre they were reluctant to try it. "When you both get home tonight," he advised, "go down to your son's room, bang on the door, and when he answers tell him to turn his music off and come upstairs because you both want to talk to him. When he finally saunters into the room with a chip on his shoulder and slumps into the kitchen chair with an attitude, look him square in the eyes and say, 'Ron, your mother and I are counting to one hundred. Now go hide.'"

When you love your son like these parents did, desperation combined with love will motivate you to try anything—even play. And one night that is what they did. Can you imagine the look on Ron's face? Can you imagine what Ron said to his friends the next day? "You guys are never going to

guess what happened last night. I played hide-and-seek with my parents until three in the morning. I still can't find them." Ron didn't become a Republican or start listening to country and western music, but when his parents played hide-and-seek with him, they did break through the long-standing tension and began the long process of healing.
                                   —Michael Yaconelli, Dangerous Wonder[1]

• • •

This may sound like an oversimplification, but the family or marriage that isn't "working" is a family or marriage that isn't playing together. Playing, using humor, having fun and building lifelong traditions are essential traits of happy, healthy, solid families. Certainly our children need to do their chores, and of course they need discipline with consistency, but what they also need desperately from their parents is a rousing game of hide-and-seek or a monthly Ping-Pong tournament.

The Perrys go out for ice cream every Monday night. The Daniel family has taken golf lessons together. The Blakes move aside all the furniture in the living room and play a family game of soccer. These are families that by no means are perfect, but they have figured out that families need a little fun to break the tension and stress of living together under the same roof.

For years, our family has taken an annual camping trip. Interestingly enough, I'm not the one who votes for camping; my wife does. When Cathy was growing up, her family camped, and it is her favorite memory of her family (even though as a teenager she complained about having to go camping).

With no offense to the female gender—or maybe it's just all the women in my life—as the only male in the family, camping is an interesting experience. Unpacking is always an event. "Rebecca, why did you bring your curling iron? There are no plugs."

"Heidi, that's a cute dress, but do you think the bears will really care?"

"Christy, I know outhouses are gross, but, yes, you will need to relieve yourself during this week—so get over it!"

As a loyal husband, I won't tell you Cathy's story, but it would have something to do with driving 87 miles to find a Starbucks while camping.

When the kids were younger, it was easier. Now camping is more difficult. They are not as excited about sleeping in a tent for a week. They don't want to leave their friends. They don't like sleeping on the ground. They don't like the food. But Cathy and I just say, "We are going anyway, and don't forget to pack your swimsuit."

The family that isn't "working" as a family isn't playing together. Playing, using humor, having fun and building lifelong traditions are essential traits of happy, healthy, solid families.

A funny thing takes place in the van on our way out of town when we stop at our favorite fast-food place, In-N-Out Burger: The kids begin to leave home behind, and although they wouldn't always admit it, they enjoy each other's company. By the time we arrive at the camping spot, they are a bit grumpy again; but after we set up camp, light the fire, eat S'mores and bring out some of the camping games that we haven't seen for a year, they forget that their blow-dryers don't work.

Every day, Cathy, the activities director, has something special planned for our family. Many days we complain about it, but by the end of the experience, we have to admit that it is fun. Then there is always splurge day. That means we rent a jet ski or go whitewater rafting or take a bike trip to a beautiful lake or go out for a nice dinner.

A funny thing happens on those camping trips: We begin to talk and laugh and lighten up. Family memories are built, inside jokes are shared and serious moments of intimacy are communicated. There are low points, too, just like in our regular weeks. But at the end of each year, usually between Christmas and New

Year's, when we take time to reflect on the year, you know what always pops up on the list of top three family experiences? It's the camping trip. Why? Because families need special times together to play together and to build lifelong memories.

Play, the Missing Ingredient

As most experts on the family will tell you, a family that prays together stays together. But I would add that a family that *plays* together will also be much more happy and healthy. For many families, play is the missing ingredient to glue the family together. Play opens closed spirits and heals broken marriages. As author Leonard Sweet puts it:

> For a marriage to sing and dance, for two people to make beautiful music together, they need to play, not work, at their marriage.[2]

Of course, there is work involved in making a marriage strong or parenting with positive results, but if you want your family to really thrive, don't forget to ask yourselves, *Are we having fun yet?*

Play Builds Family Memories

Have you ever noticed that at extended family gatherings much of the conversation is about past family experiences? "Do you remember the time Grandpa fell in the lake when we were fishing?" "I will never forget the trip we took to Disneyland" and so on. At a recent gathering of youth workers and their spouses, Cathy and I asked a purposely vague question, "What are a few of your family memories?" A minority of people in the group brought up negative memories about a divorce or some other trauma in the home; but by far, most of them recalled memories about a time their family played together or a trip their family took. We were amazed at how many of the stories were not about trips to amusement parks, but rather times together camping, traveling, fishing with Grandpa—times centered on the outdoors and fun.

When my friend Tic Long goes on a trip, his family has a motto: *No bad food, no wrong turns and no bad decisions.* Basically what they are saying is to cut loose, relax and enjoy each other's company instead of worrying about the details of the trip.

The point is to go on trips, play together and build memories—big memories and small memories. A healthy family takes time to play. Sure, it takes energy to make those memories happen, but it's worth it in our day and age when there is so much stress and pressure on families.

Play Reduces Family Stress and Tension

You are overstressed if you . . .

- Experience a continual sense of urgency and hurry or have no time to release and relax
- Have an underlying tension that causes a lot of sharp words, sibling quarrels and marital misunderstandings
- Are preoccupied with escaping, finding peace, going on vacation, quitting work or fixing family relationships
- Constantly feel frustration about getting things done
- Have a nagging desire to find a simpler life

None of these factors is unhealthy in and of itself, but when they are added together and you experience them for an extended period of time, it is time to put away your work and responsibilities and take at least an eight-day, do-nothing-but-play vacation to find some perspective. We can learn from the Europeans; their culture is much healthier than the American culture when it comes to vacations. The average European is given almost twice as many days off from work a year as the average American. How crazy we are to raise our blood pressure to dangerous heights and work our fingers to the bone, to be overcommitted and fatigued most days and then try to recuperate with a two-week vacation—only to go right back to the grind. Each of us knows deep down in our heart that something is terribly wrong with our lifestyle choices.

So lighten up and figure out a way to reduce your family's stress and tension. If you can't find eight days to relax and lighten up, take five; if you can't find five days, then take two days; if you can't find two days, see a counselor because you are either on the road to burnout, or your life and family are already a mess.

Play Produces Affirmation and Support
We know instinctively that play produces family togetherness and support. We know that when we play together, we have a deeper sense of belonging and community in the family. Parents must proactively work at making a sense of belonging and community one of their key goals for family togetherness. The following diagram illustrates the steps to family togetherness:

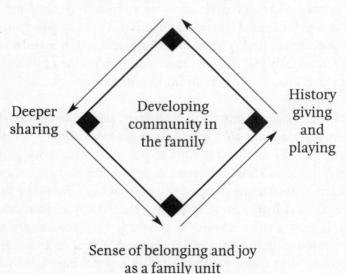

Affirmation and support

Deeper sharing

Developing community in the family

History giving and playing

Sense of belonging and joy as a family unit

The goal of family togetherness is a sense of belonging and joy, a feeling of community. Two important steps to reaching that goal are play and passing down the family history. This could be going on an outing together to Disneyland or interviewing grand-parents on what it was like to grow up on a farm. Affirmation and support are also key ingredients. With busy families and sibling rivalries, a proactive time of affirmation makes a big difference.

One of our traditions is to play the game Affirmation Bombardment on a family member's birthday. At a special dinner prepared in his or her honor, we each take a few moments to share at least three affirming thoughts about the family member whose birthday we're celebrating. This means that at least once during the year, each child is going to say something nice to her siblings. When we start Affirmation Bombardment, the kids usually roll their eyes; but every time before we're finished, the power of affirmation and support touches their heart and becomes meaningful. Parents must look for ways for the family to express affirmation and support at all times, whether through something as simple as attending each other's activities or through more formalized times of sharing like Affirmation Bombardment.

Out of history-giving and play and affirmation and support come deeper sharing. Some of the best conversations and sharing of our souls happen only after we have invested in family time. Deeper sharing causes a stronger sense of community and a more powerful sense of belonging within the family. When a family opens up and shares on an intimate level, they will meet a deep-rooted need and feel a sense of belonging and joy.

Play Causes Good Communication

My friend Bob told me a story about a season in his life when he and his son, Ryan, were struggling. Ryan had reached the magic age of 13, copped an attitude, wanted his freedom and moved his dad from the top of his priority list to somewhere right below *math word problems* and just above *chores*. The one thing they still had in common was a love for basketball.

Bob made two very good decisions to keep the communication lines open. He bought two season tickets for the local university basketball team for his son and himself. Then he went to the local Wal-Mart and brought home a basketball hoop for the driveway.

Between watching university basketball games together and almost daily playing one or two games of basketball together, Ryan and his dad kept improving the communication lines.

Bob, who is a pastor, told me that for most of that year, his son showed little to no interest in attending their church. About the same time that Dad had been demoted on the son's priority list, so had God. My friend was obviously concerned and had tried several times to have a formal talk with his son about God. But as Bob phrased it, "My son blew me off every time." Then one day in the middle of a particularly competitive game between father and son, Ryan stopped playing, looked at Bob and asked, "Dad, do you think God could love a guy like me?" Bob smiled and said, "Yes, I do think God can love a guy like you, Ryan. Now take the ball out, and we can finish this conversation after I win this game." After the game, father and son sat on the driveway and talked for an hour about spiritual issues. Bob was able to pray with his son to make a life-changing commitment to Christ.

Spontaneous communication is almost always better because it is a deposit into your child's emotional bank account.

When I asked Bob who won the game, he said, "I don't remember!"

Why is it that most of our finest conversations do not take place when we sit our children down for a big talk? Spontaneous communication is almost always better because it is a deposit into your child's emotional bank account. Usually the best mutual exchanges take place while taking a walk, playing a game, eating ice cream or doing anything fun or out of the ordinary. Educators call this "hidden curriculum"—it's almost always what takes place outside the classroom that is the best learning experience.

Playing together as a family may open up the communication lines better than anything else you try, so now is the time to be proactive and create those family fun days and events that provide the catalyst for more effective communication. Do whatever it takes to keep the communication lines open, even if it means picking up a basketball or going to the park on a regular basis. Playing together and having a good time just may be the safety net you need to make a difference in your child's life.

Humor and the Family

Humor heals broken families. A friend of mine once said, "Family jokes, though rightly cursed by strangers, are the bond that keeps most families alive." Our family has favorite funny stories about our trips that crack us up every time but can't be translated to others because "you had to be there" to get the full meaning of the story.

One of Cathy's and my goals has been to bring more comic relief to our family. With three active teenage girls in our family, life can get too intense. All five of us are strong willed, and sometimes we just take life too seriously. On the refrigerator I wrote myself a note that simply says "Lighten up!" Some of the steps that we've taken to add more comic relief include renting classic comedy movies. Once or twice a year as a family we rent certain family favorites. And when I travel, I often ask Heidi to call me and give me a joke of the day. When the family laughs together, we build a stronger bond.

Laughter is great medicine for any family. Did you know that the peak age of laughter is four? Four-year-olds laugh every four minutes, which is more than 400 times a day. Adults laugh, on average, just 15 times during an entire day. When Norman Cousins wrote the book *Anatomy of an Illness*, his premise was that humor and laughter have the power even to cure a disease—cancer, in his experience. If humor can cure an illness, then it definitely can have the power to bring families together.

Traditions and the Family

Some of the previous generations did a better job than we do with building family traditions. As I mentioned before, when extended families get together for a holiday, much of the conversation is centered around family traditions and family stories. Families tell many of the same stories year after year at these gatherings, because traditions help create family togetherness.

Planning and prioritizing make play and traditions happen. If you wait to have traditions just appear, they simply won't happen. You have to create them. Here are some ideas that you may want to begin in your family:

- *Family fun nights.* These are monthly times when the family comes together to have fun. You can do the old standbys (movies, dinner or picnics), or you can be more creative and make up your own traditions and family fun.

- *One-on-one times.* In our home, we call these "dates." These are the times when Rebecca and I go out for Mexican food or Christy and I take in a play or Heidi takes me surfing. I find that some of my most fruitful conversations with the girls happen during our monthly one-on-one times.

- *Service projects or mission trips.* Many families draw closer together and get strength from serving together. Our church sponsors family mission trips to Mexico and Ecuador—and families come back glowing. Serving together can be just the experience to develop an even stronger family bond. Our family regularly visits a local rest home and a women's shelter. These trips are worth the energy and effort.

- *Holiday traditions.* Holidays can be stressful, but if you build in special family events that become traditions, you will develop lifelong, positive memories. Fifteen years ago, we noticed that a few people from our church had nowhere to go on Christmas Eve, so we spontaneously invited them to our home after the Christmas Eve service. On the way home, I called a Chinese restaurant and ordered takeout. Every year since then, we have people over on Christmas Eve and we always order Chinese takeout. We asked our girls this past year if we should change what we eat. They were insulted!

- *Vacations and adventures.* You don't have to be rich to create great family vacations and adventures. Our kids know that every Easter vacation we will go to the beach, just like they know that each child gets to choose a family adventure when she graduates from high school.

A Commitment to Play

Todd Dean is one of my heroes. I've known him much of my adult life. He is a talented person with an M.B.A. from Stanford University. At the university, Todd had been a gymnast. When I first met him, he was teaching students from my youth group to do a standing backflip. All I could think about was liability, yet the kids loved watching him do his incredible flips. He invited me to try a backflip. I made a fool of myself, but he still encouraged me.

Todd married Charlotte. They had two beautiful children, and he had a very high-paying job. Todd's career was going through the roof, then tragedy struck: Charlotte died of a brain tumor. Before Charlotte died, Todd had told me he wanted to coach his children's Little League and soccer teams. Because Todd's career would soon include travel, he had to make some difficult decisions about his career. Todd was making good money, but it wasn't as important as playing catch with his son or rollerblading with his daughter.

Todd made the decision to quit his high-paying job and become a professor, so he could play more with his kids and coach those teams. His annual salary was cut to what was once his annual expense account. His lifestyle changed with the salary cut. He doesn't live in as large a house as he once could, and his car isn't the same model as some of his Stanford M.B.A. friends; but he is happily coaching his children's teams. He is now married to a lovely woman named Becky who suffered a similar loss. They have four happy, contented and well-adjusted children who play and interact daily with their dad and mom—who have sacrificed financially to help their family thrive. The benefits of playing together are far more valuable than a big paycheck.

DISCUSSION STARTERS

1. What fun family traditions do you remember from your childhood? What made them special?

   _____

   _____

   _____

   _____

   _____

2. What are some of your family's favorite things to do together?

   _____

   _____

   _____

   _____

   _____

3. Have you had any experiences in which playing together brought about communication with a family member? What was it?

   _____

   _____

   _____

   _____

   _____

4. What can you plan this month as a special time for the family?

_____

_____

_____

_____

_____

_____

5. How can the following Scripture apply to your family times together?

And whatever you do, whether in word or deed, do it all in the name of the Lord Jesus, giving thanks to God the Father through him (Col. 3:17).

_____

_____

_____

_____

_____

_____

_____

8

Love Your Spouse

The more a marriage is spirited and sporting, the better off for the kids. It's impossible to have a healthy family without a healthy marriage. One of the best gifts parents can bequeath to children is the example of two people in love bound together in a vibrant covenant relationship.
—*Leonard Sweet,* Learn to Dance the Soul Salsa[1]

• • •

A quality marriage is perhaps the optimum factor for rearing secure children. It has often been said that the best thing you can do for your children is to love your spouse. Sometimes that means putting your spouse's needs before your children's. Many children who grew up in a home where the parents had a child-focused marriage say they have a difficult time knowing what a good marriage looks like exactly. In other words, your greatest family investment may be your marriage.

If you are a single parent, I'll get to you at the end of this chapter; but for now, know that you can have happy, healthy children, even though it may be more difficult.

Our Story

Cathy and I have what we call a high-maintenance marriage. We met the first day of college and were married one week after Cathy graduated. Our courtship and engagement were relatively uneventful when it came to conflict, but from the moment we arrived home after a wonderful honeymoon, we began to have a great deal of it. As a pastor doing youth ministry in a church, I remember having intense arguments with Cathy on the way to our youth-group meeting and then standing up in front of the kids, feeling like a hypocrite. What made things worse was that during that season in the Church, people didn't talk much about marital conflict, so I thought we were the only ones out there with problems. I remember so well when one leader in our congregation told us that he and his wife had never had a fight. Never! My reaction was a deep sense of guilt. Yet now, years later, I feel deeply sorry for them. Conflict and intimacy tend to go hand in hand.

Perhaps our greatest marriage lesson came about five years into our union. After a year of marital unbliss, we moved from California to Princeton, New Jersey, where we attended graduate school. The Princeton years were actually better than our first year of marriage, but we still needed improvement. We both realized we didn't have the communication tools we needed in order to work on our high-maintenance marriage.

A quality marriage is perhaps the optimum factor for rearing secure children. Your greatest family investment may be your marriage.

After graduate school, we moved to Orange, California, where Cathy started teaching and I began a youth-ministry program at a church. We became very busy. Cathy worked as a teacher by day and was my number-one adult volunteer for the youth group by night. Our days, nights, mornings and evenings were a blur of activity with the youth group. Our youth ministry grew from four kids on the first Sunday to more than 100 in just three months, and the numbers just kept on growing. With numerical growth came loads of affirmation for me. After the first year, the church actually doubled my salary. We counted that as at least as great a miracle as Jesus' walking on water! We bought our first house, and I thought life was going great. My entire being was focused on my work, which gave me enthusiasm and self-esteem.

One night after a particularly excellent evening with the students, Cathy said, "Jim, we need to talk." I could see she was very serious, but being the dense male that I can be, I thought she wanted to talk about a problem with one of the kids in the youth group. At the time, we were basically running a MASH unit for kids and families in crisis. Helping families succeed was my theme, and judging by the number of people participating in our program, we could tell we were prospering. Now Cathy and I were sitting across from each other at the Salt and Pepper Restaurant, which was open 24 hours a day.

"Jim, I feel abandoned by you. I feel resentment every time the phone rings or you are gone one more night. I know how you will probably respond, and you are partly right—God has been doing a special work in our ministry. But, Jim, I'm even beginning to resent God."

Cathy had me pegged. Yes, we were gloriously out of control—but all with good things. It's true that there had been little focus on our marriage and intimacy was ebbing. I would come home after a very busy, successful and stressful day and crash, only to get up and do it all over again the next day. Cathy went on to say, "I feel like you are having an affair. I can't imagine how you would find the time, but you sure aren't investing in our relationship."

I knew she was right. Cathy had even taken away my ammunition; I couldn't blame it all on God, who was blessing our youth ministry. So I just said, "You're right. Not about the affair, but about the focus not being on our marriage."

Neither of us had had very good role models in our lives in the areas of courtship, intimacy and healthy relationships. We spent the next hour trying to figure out what to do. Was it time to quit my beloved work? How could we have the children we wanted with this kind of lifestyle and pace? We were embarrassed to talk with anyone and really share how bad it was.

At that table, in the midst of our immaturity and lack of knowledge, we made three decisions that we hoped would stop our marriage from continuing on its rocky course:

1. Nonnegotiable date night
2. Only out three nights a week
3. Cathy to have veto power over the schedule

These three decisions were our action steps. I looked forward to the date night idea, but I didn't know how we would find the time. The decision to work toward only being out working three nights a week felt awfully oppressive, but I knew I needed to take a drastic measure. And the veto power over the schedule was almost a passive-aggressive act on my part to appease Cathy's concerns. I saw it as a bit of an overreaction to her critique of our marriage. And yet, those three decisions proved to be lifesavers for our marriage and good boundaries when children became part of our lives.

Because these guidelines have worked so well for Cathy and me, I'd like you to consider trying them out in your marriage. But before you decide, let me tell you the rest of our story.

Nonnegotiable Date Nights

Cathy and I don't miss many date nights. We know that even though life can get overly busy and we often get distracted, at least once a week we are going to stop what we are doing and focus on each other. Most of our dates aren't very expensive. In fact, when our children were younger, the cost of a baby-sitter was sometimes more expensive than the date. The date is not a time to talk about the bills or the kids' school plans; it's a time to focus on each other. It's not a time to let down; it's a time to make some positive deposits into each other's emotional wellbeing. Cathy can handle a busy schedule as long as she knows that there will be a sanctuary of love, support and focus on our weekly date night. (Date mornings and date afternoons are good, too, by the way.)

When Cathy and I celebrated our twenty-fifth wedding anniversary, we sent the kids to camp and took a very special trip. Knowing they were safe and having a good time, we were actually glad to be away from the kids; and yet, we spent much of our time talking about them. So much of our focus was on them. On extended trips, this is fine—unless you wake up one day and realize that you have nothing in common with your spouse except for the kids or that one or both of you have given all your energy to priorities other than each other.

At Home Together

We decided to be out only three nights each week. There is nothing magical about the number three; it just works for us. The average pastor in America is out five nights a week. Cathy and I can't function as well with that much time away from home. You have to learn what works for you as a couple and family and then make decisions to constantly bring health and renewal to the relationship.

When Rebecca was 14, one of her friends was over for dinner before youth group. We sat down at the table for a rushed meal, but we were all together. Her friend commented, "This is so nice. I can't remember the last time our family sat around the kitchen table for dinner!" Interestingly enough, the girl's mother had just confided to Cathy and me that life was extremely difficult at home. A few more nights a week together won't necessarily take away all your problems, but this discipline has been a godsend for our family.

Veto Power Over the Schedule

Once Cathy and I took those three action steps, the calendar became one of our biggest nightmares and bones of contention. Some of our most intense disagreements were about the schedule that Cathy had not bought into. When I first gave Cathy veto power over my schedule, I only saw it as a control agent for her and a negative for me. I was wrong.

Today we do the calendar together, and we seldom—if ever—argue or blame each other about it. Cathy tends to be more aware of the details of the family schedule. I have a tendency to say yes to everything, and she guards me from me. There are times when we grieve together our decisions that have brought a hectic time into our lives, but because we both made the decisions, it's easier not to blame the other person.

The Spark

Over time, every couple's relationship can become predictable. Romance, sex and even conversation can become routine or non-existent. If "routine" or "predictable" sums up your situation, then it's time to refocus some of your energy on your spouse. If your relationship is suffering due to lack of attention, here are some questions to help you evaluate what needs to happen to light the spark again:

1. When you and your spouse were dating before you were married, what did you do to make him or her feel special?
2. What are you doing right now to make your mate feel special?
3. What was the last fun activity you and your spouse did together?
4. How often do you participate in activities you both enjoy?
5. If you asked your spouse to list your top five priorities based on where you devote the most time and effort, what would those priorities be?
6. Where does your spouse rank on that list?

These questions might be a good start to get the dialog moving in the right direction and fan the flames so that they burn brighter than ever.

Most of the couples I know tell me that they love each other but that they're just too busy with their work, kids and all the activities they're juggling. All of their time is focused on good things, but they have neglected their marriage. They hope to make some changes in the near future, but *now* is the time to make the important decisions.

Ron and Susan are the perfect illustration of a couple who mean well but have discovered that their marriage is suffering because they are just too busy. Ron is a policeman. Susan is a preschool teacher. She teaches because they need the money, but it also works well with their three children's schedules. They put all of their schedules on the computer; with soccer, ballet, school, church, jobs, music lessons and much more, their lives are pretty complicated. By the time the kids get to bed, Ron and Susan are too tired to relate to each other; and when they are tired and stressed, they tend to argue more than relate. Ron's replenishing relationships are with his fellow police officers, and Susan gets her support from her mother, who lives in another city, and a couple of the teachers from her school.

They confided in me that although things looked great on the outside, they were very worried that their marriage was crumbling from the inside out. I asked what I thought was a simple question: "What areas of your busy life can you cut back on, so you can re-focus your energy on each other?"

They went through a litany of activities that would make any-one tired. They concluded with "There is absolutely nothing we can change."

"What about jobs?" I asked.

"We need the money," they insisted.

"What about all the kids' activities?" I continued.

"We can't change a thing. Neither of us had the opportunity to do all this stuff, and we want our kids to enjoy every activity they can."

I had to tell them the painful truth. "Then it looks like those beautiful, busy kids of yours will be excellent soccer players and musicians but have parents who don't like each other very much." They didn't appreciate my comment.

The answer for Ron and Susan, and maybe you, is to cut back and do less. To find the time to replenish your relationship, you might need to cut something out of your busy schedule. Can I let you in on a secret? Kids would rather have parents who like each other than learn how to play one more musical instrument or score another goal in soccer. I'm not telling you to back off com-pletely, but just find a rhythm for your family that works for everyone, including you and your spouse, and that is healthy for your marriage.

Romance

There is a significant drop in satisfaction in a couple's romance and sex lives when children arrive on the scene. However, couples with the most positive families make sex and romance a priority. Don't let kids, money, busyness or anything else rob you of romance. When I kiss Cathy in front of my kids, they act like they're grossed out, but really they like it. It gives them security. The only way to make romance a priority is to schedule it on the calendar. Sure, a scheduled date night is not as spontaneous as your romantic activities were before you had children; but if you don't schedule special times together, they probably won't happen often enough.

Two Scripture verses from the New Testament are meaningful to me in this area. Ephesians 5:25 says, "Love your wives." The actual Greek meaning is "Keep on loving [or even treasuring] your wives." This goes for wives also. The other verse is not just about marriage, but it is one of our marriage's foundation verses: "Outdo one another in showing honor" (Rom. 12:10, *NRSV*). When we try to treat our spouse as a king or queen, it shows our spouse that we care. Cathy likes to say, "Romance starts in the morning with how we treat each other throughout the day."

Spiritual Intimacy

Here's an interesting observation. Never in all my years of ministering to youth and families and counseling couples have I ever encountered a couple that prayed together *and* experienced serious difficulties. Nor have I ever known a couple that, once they had agreed to pray together and stuck to it, ended up getting a divorce. Praying together restores balance and priorities in a marriage because it recognizes that God loves both partners equally. Furthermore, bringing a disagreement before the bar of ultimate justice removes it somehow from the influence of human bitterness. People change their tone of voice when they pray, and it becomes almost impossible to remain argumentative.

Marriage experts Les and Leslie Parrott reported a recent study that showed that couples that attend church, even as little as once a month, increase their chances of staying married for life. Studies also show that churchgoers feel better about their marriages than those who don't worship together. Further research shows that the happiest couples are those that pray together. Couples that pray together are twice as likely as those that don't to describe their marriages as being highly romantic. And according to the Parrotts, married couples that pray together are 90 percent more likely to report higher satisfaction with their sex lives than couples who don't.[2] Prayer draws couples and families closer together. It's like the young couple that decided to start their honeymoon by kneeling beside their bed to pray. The bride giggled when she heard her new husband's prayer: "For what we are about to receive, may the Lord make us truly thankful!"

One of the common themes in the temptation narratives of the Bible is isolation. That's why for Cathy's and my spiritual betterment and growth as a couple, we choose to be in a regular couples' Bible study as well as our own same-sex support groups. Who replenishes your relationships spiritually? Are you proactively seeking out mentors to help you grow spiritually, both as a marriage partner and as an individual? Do you have a regular daily time with God in prayer and devotion? Do you ever take time as a couple to participate in a couples' retreat at your church or in one of the many programs offered around the country to enhance your marriage and your spiritual life?

About once a month, I do a marriage conference somewhere around the world. It is one of the most enjoyable and fruitful parts of my life. At each conference, I offer couples the "Closer Challenge." This challenge is based on Cathy's and my many years of failure to draw together toward spiritual intimacy. Call it busyness, distraction, spiritual warfare or a combination of all three, but we tried every kind of book or program. We always started off well and then quickly faded. One day a mentor of ours said, "Why don't you try making an appointment with each other once a week?" We did. It took the pressure off and drew us closer together spiritually. We now have a book out called *Closer* that challenges couples to take 20 to 30 minutes together a week. We challenge couples to read Scripture, focus on a topic and then dialog about the topic and pray together. We have never met a couple who has taken on the Closer Challenge who has not benefited from it.

Ongoing Communication

Cathy and I do not feel that, as we were growing up, we had excellent role models when it came to communicating. We inherited some of the same poor communication habits of our parents and even our grandparents. We've laughed that if my father and Cathy's mother were to get married, it would be the beginning of World War III. And then we pause for a moment and realize that in many ways, when it comes to communication styles, they did get married—in us!

When Cathy and I were first married, we made the mistake of never discussing the topic of finances. I assumed that I would handle them; after all, my father never allowed my mother to touch the checkbook. On the other hand, Cathy's mom handled the finances in her home, and she expected to do the same. Cathy is a detail person. The bank statement must balance to the penny, even if it takes her all night. I am much more comfortable rounding off everything to the nearest $10 and moving on to something more fun. You can imagine the conflict that started when "her mom" and "my dad" met over the finances. It wasn't a pretty sight. Cathy would get upset, and I would get my feelings hurt; then we would move from finances to anything else that was bugging us. Before we knew it, neither of us liked each other very much anymore.

How does a high-maintenance marriage like ours, between two people with poor communication skills, survive? You have to work at it every day. As you work on your communication skills, not only are you assuring your marriage's success, but you are also modeling for your children how to communicate, so their future relationships will have a better chance as well. I'll tell you about a few rules that work for us.

"After 10:30 P.M." Rule

I get up early. Cathy is a night owl. I'm the guy who, while Cathy and I were praying together one night, fell asleep in the middle of my own prayer! By default, Cathy always has the advantage in conflicts occurring after 10:30 P.M., and I automatically win the battles waged before 8:00 A.M. We know that for good communication or for conflict resolution to take place, we do better before 10:30 P.M. and not in the middle of the pit hours of preparation for dinner, homework, bedtime for the kids and all the other things that we have to face between 6:00 P.M. and 9:00 P.M. We also know it is almost worthless to communicate before our kids go to school. These boundaries and expectations help us find times when we can focus on each other and are in a better place and frame of mind.

"It's More Difficult in Bed" Rule

In my opinion, the marriage bed is sacred; it's for sleeping and, uh, you know. If Cathy and I need to meet about the kids or discuss a potential conflict, we have found the bed not to be the place most conducive to communication. I fall asleep, and that makes Cathy frustrated. We have found that if we regularly schedule a Burns-family business meeting, we can use that time to take care of the business-type issues of the family. This is where we try to discuss the schedule, insurance problems, finances, car needs, house needs and all the rest of the stuff it takes to run a family.

Most couples do not have a set time each week to meet, so the business issues are often brought up at an inappropriate time or place or put off indefinitely.

Most couples do not have a set time each week to meet, so the business issues are often brought up at an inappropriate time or place or put off indefinitely. I don't know about you, but the weekly business meeting isn't my favorite time with my spouse.

However, it is one of our most important hours of the week, and it keeps us from having to deal with the business issues on our date night, during our times of spiritual growth together or when we're on the run.

"Take Your Temperature Before You Have a Fever" Rule

You might call this rule the preventative medicine rule. Do you and your spouse schedule times of extended communication so that you can take a longer look at the needs of your marriage and family life?

In chapter 3, I described one of Dave and Pam Hicks' secrets to a healthy family. Cathy and I now follow their example and take a day away every six months to focus on our kids. We try to make a fun day out of it—we go out for a nice lunch or spend the day at the beach. With pens and notebooks in hand, we examine the areas of our children's lives that we believe are crucial for us as parents to be very present in; and we discuss, make plans and create an agenda for each child for the coming six months. We talk about what we hope to teach each child in the areas of morals and values, school issues, relationships, friendships, health issues and especially spiritual growth. We close our time by praying for each child and for our ability to remain firm in our biblical convictions on parenting. Even though Cathy and I have disagreed over a parenting position many times, our parenting retreats are always well worth the time. They definitely have made us better, more proactive parents who focus on prevention rather than allow our children to be reared by chance.

Cathy and I also make a habit of going away for a few days right around our anniversary, not only to celebrate the year, but also to evaluate our marriage. Some years it's been a wonderful exercise in positive communication, and other times we've had to ask, "How did we get through this year still liking each other?"

A couple of memorable getaways come to mind. One year, Cathy planned the whole trip. It was just one night away, but we really needed it. She enjoyed surprising me with an overnight at a bed-and-breakfast overlooking beautiful Lake Arrowhead in the

Southern California mountains. We had a great dinner and a great night.

Cathy didn't want to be distracted, so after we checked out of the bed-and-breakfast, she rented a rowboat. As we sat in the middle of the lake, she handed me a sheet she'd prepared that listed 10 needs of couples. She asked me to rank in order, from most important to least important, what I thought her needs were and then rank my own needs on the other side of the page. Three hours later, we were still discussing how to meet each other's needs more effectively. You may want to borrow the same idea. The list of the 10 key needs of a husband and wife originated with Willard Harley, Jr., in his book *His Needs, Her Needs*:

- Sexual fulfillment
- Recreational companionship
- An attractive spouse
- Domestic support
- Admiration
- Affection
- Conversation
- Honesty and openness
- Financial support
- Family commitment[3]

A strong marriage definitely takes a great deal of work. However, when you look at the vitality it brings to your entire family, you'll agree that the work is well worth it. Is your marriage a child-focused marriage? Marriages that are totally child-focused don't work well and, most of the time, don't last. Your children want and need you to invest time and effort in your marriage. Even if they complain about date nights or extended times away that you and your spouse take, in their hearts they know that you and your spouse need time alone.

A good marriage will bring much security to a child. If it has been awhile since you and your spouse took the time to focus on each other instead of the kids, then don't delay. Now is the time to put the needs of the kids aside for a brief period to strengthen the emotional, physical and spiritual bonds that once firmly held you and your spouse together.

You can find many helpful marriage resources at Home Word.com, including *Creating an Intimate Marriage* and *Closer*, written with my wife, Cathy.

A Word to Single Parents

If you are a single parent and you have stayed with me through this chapter, then you probably have some mixed feelings about the content. When I speak at single parents' groups, I am reminded of what incredible people single parents are and the extra load they carry. Parenting is tough enough with two people, let alone with only one.

I'd like to share with you a story from the Bible: Moses and the Israelites were battling their archenemy, the Amalekites. God instructed Moses to hold his arms up high above his head with his staff in his hand. When Moses kept his arms raised, the Israelites would begin to win the battle; but when he grew tired and he dropped his arms, the Amalekites would start to win the battle. Finally, when Moses was exhausted, others stood beside him and helped him hold his arms high. The Israelites ended up winning the battle because of the helpers Moses used to keep his arms held high (see Exod. 17:8-16).

Who comes alongside you to help you with your children when you get tired or lose perspective along the way? Are you discouraged and too tired to fight some of the battles that need to be fought? All parents—especially single parents—have to find the courage to ask for help and find replenishing relationships for themselves and their children. The church is a very good place to seek out some of those replenishing relationships.

Mary, a friend of ours, is a single parent and my pick for Mother of the Year. She is a networker. She finds others whom she can serve and who can serve her family needs. She has chosen to be involved in her church, where many of the moms take care of each other and look after the needs of each other's children. She can't afford fancy vacations or even much time off from work, but on a shoestring budget she still manages to create family fun nights and vacation traditions that will make wonderful memories for her children. Her life hasn't turned out the way she had dreamed it would, but she is constantly on the lookout for ways to focus on the positive and for people like her church's youth workers who can help her bring up her children to be responsible adults.

No one said it would be easy, but with God's help and by finding the right people to come alongside you, your kids will thrive.

DISCUSSION STARTERS

1. Were your parents positive or negative role models for a healthy marriage?

   _____

   _____

   _____

   _____

2. Do you agree or disagree with the following statement by Billy Graham? Why?

   If couples would put half the effort into marriage that they put into courtship, they would be surprised how things would brighten up.[4]

   _____

   _____

   _____

   _____

   _____

3. Which areas of your marriage need improving? Which areas are doing well?

_____

_____

_____

_____

_____

_____

4. How does the following Scripture apply to your marriage?

Submit to one another out of reverence for Christ (Eph. 5:21).

_____

_____

_____

_____

_____

_____

5. For further conversations, read Ephesians 5:22-33. Discuss the concepts of submission to each other and submission to God.

_____

_____

_____

_____

_____

_____

Communication Issues and Questions

Here are other communication tools that have worked for us.

A. Discuss These Issues with Your Spouse, Topic by Topic
    Goals, thoughts, worries, hopes and dreams
    Our relationship
    The ministry
    Spiritual growth
    Sex
    Family
      · Children
      · In-laws
      · Each other
    Finances
    Education
    Physical health
    Spouse's needs
    Fears
    Other issues

B. Complete These Sentences
    Sometimes I become blocked in our relationship when . . .
    Sometimes I feel angry when . . .
    Sometimes when I am happy, I . . .
    One of the things I wish you knew more about me is . . .
    If I could be sure no one would laugh at me . . .
    Ever since I was a child . . .

C. The Five Languages of Love

    · Words of affirmation
    · Quality time
    · Receiving gifts
    · Acts of service
    · Physical touch

1. What are your two primary languages of love?
2. What are your spouse's two primary languages of love?
3. Specify what you can do to communicate love in your spouse's love language.

D. Making Love Last Forever

Be sure you are making more deposits than withdrawals into your spouse's emotional wellbeing. A *deposit* is anything positive and security-producing that gives your mate energy. A *withdrawal* is anything sad or negative that drains energy from your mate.

1. In what ways can you make more deposits into your spouse's account?
2. What deposits do you wish you could receive from your spouse?
3. Identify ways you are making withdrawals from your spouse's account.

The Best Things in Life Are Not Things

Dear Dad,

$chool i$ really great. I am making lot$ of friend$ and $tudying very hard. With all my $tuff, I $imply can't think of anything I need, $o if you would like, you can ju$t $end me a card, a$ I would love to hear from you.

Love,
Your $on

Dear Son,

I kNOw that astroNOmy, ecoNOmics and oceaNOgraphy are eNOugh to keep even an hoNOr student busy. Do NOt forget that the pursuit of kNOwledge is a NOble task, and you can never study eNOugh.

Love,
Dad

• • •

For a number of years, Cathy and I gave our daughters money each semester for a clothes allowance. With this income, they could choose to buy whatever clothing they wanted (within reason), but it was all the money they would receive for clothes for the semester.

Christy had it figured out: She looked for sales and was quite the bargain shopper. On the other hand, Rebecca chooses more expensive clothes and did spur-of-the-moment shopping. (In our family, Christy shops like Mom and Rebecca shops like Dad!) One time, I saw Christy wearing Rebecca's new expensive skirt, which she hadn't yet worn. I asked Christy if she had Rebecca's permission, and she told me that Rebecca had sold it to her for half price. Why would she do that? Because Rebecca had spent her entire clothing allowance and had forgotten to purchase shoes! She had asked Mom to bail her out. Mom offered a small loan, but Rebecca chose to sell her skirt to get new shoes.

Rebecca learned a lesson that many kids don't learn until adulthood: There is only so much money to go around, and the decisions you make about how you spend it will either benefit you, or strap you and add more pressure than you want or need.

Money and Stewardship

Let's face it: Money is a problem for most families; most of us do not have as much as we want. Families are often more focused on money problems than they would like to be. I think it is partly because of poor decision making and planning. Families with a huge weight of debt are families who struggle. Families who handle their money properly—whether they are rich, poor or in-between— are much happier and healthier. Money may not be able to buy you love, but it is one of the most common sources of conflict in marriages and one of the missing topics when learning about parenting for positive results. Perhaps the most sobering financial statistic of all is the Gallup poll finding that 56 percent of all divorces are the result of financial tension in the home![1]

Money is one of the most common sources of conflict in marriages and one of the missing topics when learning about parenting for positive results.

When I worked in the church as a youth pastor, I realized that people didn't like the pastor to speak about money. They would say it is a private and personal topic, but Jesus sure didn't have a problem talking about money. The Bible says a great deal about it; scholars tell us that there are around 500 verses on prayer, 500 verses on faith and more than 2,350 verses on money!

Whether we like it or not, much of our world and our family decisions revolve around money. This definitely doesn't mean that materialism is the answer to family problems. On the contrary, our focus on finances will be a major determining factor for a successful family as well as for the financial health and stewardship of our children and family.

I have spent much of my life living in affluent areas of the country, yet some of the most unhealthy and unhappy families I have ever known come from neighborhoods with mortgages and lease payments that most of us can hardly imagine. This may not sound politically correct, but some of the healthiest families I've ever met are on the east coast of communist Cuba. These families live under an oppressed government, and their monthly income is as little as $14. Materially they have very little, but they have learned to live contented, beautiful lives. They understand the spiritual concept of stewardship much better than some of my wealthier friends whose families are falling apart.

The decisions we make as parents about our financial health often play a major factor in our family's overall lifestyle. Jesus summarized it so well in the Sermon on the Mount: "For where your treasure is, there your heart will be also" (Matt. 6:21). A few sentences later in that most incredible sermon, He went on to challenge His listeners with these words: "No one can serve two masters. Either he will hate the one and love the other, or he will be devoted to the one and despise the other. You cannot serve both God and Money" (v. 24).

Basically there are two economic value systems battling for our family's soul. The world's value system places emphasis on things and stuff. God's value is invested in people, stewardship and beauty. The problem lies in the fact that the world system influences all of us; the balance of money and things of the Spirit is not only a problem for parents but for children as well. According to Jesus, we pay most of our attention to whatever we treasure. Our hearts are drawn to our treasure.

I like the story my pastor told of a Catholic priest who was approached by thieves who came into his beautiful cathedral to steal some of its valuable treasures. With a gun pointed at the head of the priest, they said, "Show us your valuable treasures." He agreed. They walked into the cathedral, past the golden altar and out the back door. He pointed to a group of 20 orphans playing ball in the back. He said, "These are the treasures of this cathedral."

The answer to the money-pit issue is to be a faithful steward of your resources. Financial counselors Ron and Judy Blue define stewardship as "the use of God-given resources for the accomplishment of God-given goals."[2] The Blues list four stewardship principles to live by:

1. God owns it all.
2. There is always a trade-off between time and effort and money and rewards.
3. There is no such thing as an "independent financial decision."
4. Delayed gratification is the key to financial maturity.[3]

Stewardship is a spiritual issue. Someone once said that a man or woman can enrich his or her bank account at the expense of empowering his or her soul. Martin Luther is known to have said that a person cannot be truly converted unless his or her heart, mind *and pocketbook* are converted. Isn't it true that the amount of light that gets into any room depends on the state of the window through which the light must pass? With this in mind, the light that gets into our soul depends on our focus.

For many, what we focus on is what we become. I asked a group of teenagers what they wanted to be when they grew up. I received all kinds of answers: attorney, pastor, homemaker, teacher, businessperson. One 14-year-old, Jerry, simply said, "I want to be rich."

"Okay, Jerry," I replied, "but what do you want to be? What kind of job? What do you want to do?"

He shot right back, "You don't understand. I don't care what I do. I just want to be wealthy. I want a large home overlooking the water, with a boat and a Porsche."

I came back at him and simply said, "I think your goals are too low. Success is not spelled M-O-N-E-Y." Unfortunately, Jerry's parents had planted in his brain the misconception that only wealthy people are happy. Sorry, Jerry; it's not as much about money as you've been taught. I like what my father used to say: "The best things in life are not things!"

Basic Financial Principles

A family consumed with money problems is often a family that somewhere along the road made a wrong turn. As stated earlier, money issues are always one of the top reasons for divorce. Money problems reach up to the richest of the rich and also show up in pastors' homes. Money is on the minds of people living on skid row as well as those working in the financial district two blocks down the street.

A family consumed with money problems is often one that somewhere along the road made a wrong turn.

Cathy and I don't always excel at stewardship. We, like most Christians, are trying. We're improving. Sometimes Cathy and I speak at seminars on ministry and marriage. Like ourselves, ministry couples often have to work extra hard to maintain a healthy marriage and family. When we speak at these seminars, we almost always bring up the issue of finances. We only plan for a few minutes on this topic, but it never fails to become one of the major areas of interest for pastors and their spouses.

Spend Less Than You Make
"Spend less than you make." When we first started speaking on finances, we actually threw that line in for comic relief. We thought the audience would laugh. They didn't. They got serious and wrote it down in their notes. Why? Because most Americans don't. At

last count, individuals in America alone owe more than $3.5 trillion.[4] We have so much personal debt in our country that the average person has been described as someone driving on a bond-financed highway, in a bank-financed car, fueled by charge-card-financed gasoline, going to purchase furniture on the installment plan to put in his savings-and-loan-financed home! The fact is that we are drowning in a sea of debt, and we are bound to have serious financial, spiritual and family casualties. However, there is an answer. Go against the grain of our culture and have the discipline to spend less than you make.

A Budget Is a Must

In one of the most popular financial books of the 1990s, *The Millionaire Next Door,* the authors set out to find the millionaires in our country and document what they do and how they make their money. The authors were shocked at what they discovered. The millionaires didn't all live in the most expensive houses. They were people who lived fairly ordinary lives with a couple of key principles that brought them wealth. Although they followed the principle "spend less than you make," the most common ingredient was that they lived with a budget.

If you don't have a budget, you cannot possibly know if you are winning or losing the debt war. A budget is a map to help you stay on track with your finances and be a faithful steward of the resources God has given you.

Debt Is Slavery

Credit, interest and debt are just poor stewardship. Take Del and Elaine for example. They buy two brand-new mountain bikes for $475 apiece. With tax, their investment is a little more than $1,000. They put their new purchase on a credit card that offers 18 percent interest. Two years later, they are still paying for the bikes they have ridden only twice, and now the cost of the bikes is approximately $1,400.

Here's what the Bible says about debt: "The rich rule over the poor, and the borrower is servant to the lender" (Prov. 22:7). With debt, you literally become a slave to the lender. Deuteronomy 28:1-2 tells us:

If you fully obey the LORD your God and carefully follow all his commands I give you today, the LORD your God will set you high above all the nations on earth. All these blessings will come upon you and accompany you if you obey the LORD your God.

Debt even extracts a physical toll. Debt often increases stress, which contributes to mental, physical and emotional fatigue, which in turn stifles creativity and harms relationships.

Debt extracts a physical toll. Debt often increases stress, which contributes to mental, physical and emotional fatigue, which in turn stifles creativity and harms relationships.

Delayed Gratification Is the Answer

What would have been the better use of Del and Elaine's money? As much as they desired the bikes, they didn't have the cash to buy them, so they should have waited. They either could have developed a savings plan for the bikes, or "bike fever" would have gone away and they would not be strapped with a huge bill and no place to put the bikes that they seldom use.

Children see; children do. If you ask a five-year-old boy (or girl) whether he would like a double-decker ice cream on a hot day or a $50 savings bond for college, which do you think he would take? No doubt, the ice cream. However, after years of watching his parents make delayed gratification decisions, he will eventually begin to get it.

Give 10 Percent, Save 10 Percent

This may be an oversimplification, but I have never met anyone who consistently has tithed on his or her income and saved another 10 percent of his or her income *and* has had a major financial problem. Back to the millionaires next door: They probably acquired their wealth through the miracle of compound interest and a drastic savings program. Hopefully these same people took seriously the biblical mandate of the tithe and applied it to their lives as well.

Several years ago, I helped run the annual stewardship campaign for our church. It was an enlightening experience to say the least. A few of us read the pledge cards, so for that season I was in the know regarding who gave what to the church. It was a most humbling experience. As I looked at the families who were generous with their gifts, I noticed that they were by no means the wealthiest. I noticed something else: They were many of the healthiest families in our congregation.

If you don't currently have a savings plan,
start small, but start this week.

If you don't currently have a savings plan, start small, but start this week. If you don't regularly give a percentage of your income back to God, then start today. It's a great reminder that all of your treasure ultimately comes from Him.

Faithful Stewardship

Howard Dayton is a friend and hero of mine who started a wonderful organization called Crown Ministries. Crown takes the concept of financial stewardship and trains thousands of men and women to be faithful with their financial resources. I have called Crown a healing-and-deliverance mission for the vast number of people who need to be set free from financial bondage.

Years ago, Howard created a diagram that helps us keep the goal of faithful financial stewardship in mind.[5] You can use the diagram on the following page to evaluate your own stewardship and as a goal to work toward. I keep it close to my heart as I look at our own finances and as I seek to fulfill my responsibility to train our children in this most important, but often overlooked, area.

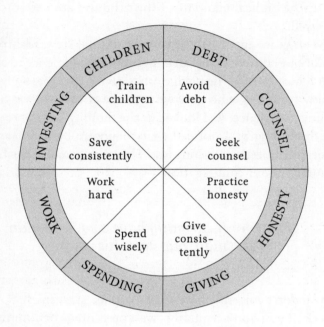

Take a look at each area of the diagram, and rate how you are doing as a faithful steward of your finances. Next, rank each area of the diagram from 1 to 5 below (1 = "doing well," 5 = "needs immediate attention"), and make a decision to improve where needed.

___ Avoiding debt
___ Seeking counsel
___ Practicing honesty
___ Giving generously
___ Spending wisely
___ Working hard
___ Saving consistently
___ Training children

Financial Education for Children

If a couple doesn't have a proactive training process for their children's morals and values, then they probably won't be doing much to train their children to handle finances in a right way either. It's probably because the couple themselves still have a great deal of work to do in both areas. So learn together. That's what our family has done.

Cathy and I realized that, although we might receive higher marks on the financial stewardship report card than some people, we did not do a good job of teaching our children about it. It came to a head one day when our oldest was about seven years old. She thought that if you needed something, all you had to do was go to the ATM and get money out. She was shocked to hear that you actually first had to put money in the bank in order to get it out.

Here are a few questions to consider:

1. Does our family have a stewardship philosophy? Can our children articulate our family's stewardship agenda?
2. Do our children know the power of giving?
3. Do they understand the emptiness of materialism and the benefits of delayed gratification?
4. Have we given them charge of some area of their financial lives to teach them personal responsibility? (Obviously, this must be age-appropriate.)

Teach Your Children About Stewardship

It is never too early to introduce the biblical concept of stewardship to children. As children move from dependence on us to independence, the lessons they learn about stewardship will help prepare them for adulthood in one of the most important ways possible. If you haven't done much work with your children in this area, then there is no better time to start than now.

What is your family's stewardship philosophy? One family we know discussed it with their kids and came up with the following paragraph:

Our material possessions are actually on loan to us from God. We acknowledge His generous love and gifts to us. We will be a family who looks for ways to give generously, stays out of debt except for our house and car, and realizes that everything we have is on loan from God anyway.

Another family borrowed a quote they ran across: "When it comes to money, small things are small things, but faithfulness with small things is a big thing." They went on to write, "We will faithfully look for ways to faithfully give back to God." Our family uses the diagram from Howard Dayton. We fill in specifics for our family in each of the areas, and then we review the goals. Another idea is to teach children to live by Ron and Judy Blue's stewardship principles.

When it comes to money, small things are small things, but faithfulness with small things is a big thing.

Consider Your Children's Allowance to Be Their Paycheck

We like the idea of a regular payday. Some people give their children an allowance on the day they receive their paycheck; we give our kids theirs weekly. Allowances are the first step in learning money management. Look at an allowance as a mini-salary that helps young people learn how to handle money. A good rule is to begin giving children a small allowance when they must learn some money management skills, usually around first grade. As the children get older, give them more allowance for more responsibility; and by the time they leave the house, they should be handling almost all their purchases and budgeting.

Teach Your Children Early to Save and Tithe

Most kids have trouble with the concepts of saving and tithing. But the concept isn't difficult just for kids—few American adults save and tithe! I suggest that you find a bank with low- or no-fee passbook accounts and open one for each of your children. Let them watch the interest grow. Establish some goals for savings, and help keep them accountable to meet their savings goals.

Cathy and I have not gone broke with our offer of matching dollar-for-dollar whatever our girls save or give. It has been a good way to encourage the power of saving and giving. We let our daughters help make decisions on some of our discretionary giving to charity, missions and the church. Our kids sponsor two Compassion International children, whom we have watched grow up and mature. Our children write to their Compassion children and are excited when they receive letters back.

Help Your Children Understand the Positive Power of a Budget
Most couples who come to my office for premarital counseling are surprised when I tell them that I won't meet with them again unless they show me a simple budget before the next session. Most of them have never put together a budget, and I usually have to coach them or offer them one of the many outstanding resources by Howard Dayton, Ron Blue or Larry Burkett, to name a few of the excellent financial stewardship gurus today.

You don't have to make your children's budget complicated. In fact, the simpler the budget, the better.

You don't have to make your children's budget complicated. In fact, the simpler the budget, the better. When your children are in elementary school, a budget may look as simple as giving, saving and spending. As they get older and you give them more financial responsibilities, you can break down the spending categories: school activities, personal grooming, entertainment, clothing and gifts.

If you ask your teenagers to create a monthly spending journal as well, it will be a great addition to the budget and will help them realize exactly what they are spending—or wasting—their money on.

Sample Monthly Journal

Month:
Opening Balance: $47.50

Date	Description	Income	Expenses	Balance
1/13	Allowance	3.00		50.50
1/15	Baby-sitting	10.00		60.50
1/16	Gift to the church	5.00		55.50
1/20	Movie and snacks	13.00		42.50
1/24	Gift from Aunt Ann	20.00		62.50
1/24	Makeup		3.50	59.00
1/28	Bowling		7.00	52.00
1/29	T-shirt		18.00	34.00

Closing Balance: $34.00

Some red on fi-
nances. A ies whose
children they had
plenty of of money
offers yo ewardship
and it in iance.

As v d to teach
our chil that a wise
old bus

A y r of his
con become
wis "

 ertainly,
my son—two words."

The young man said, "Please tell me, sir, what are those
two words?"

The wise old man said, " 'Good decisions.' "

The young man thought about this and then said boldly, "Sir, can you tell me how you learn to make good decisions about finances?"

The wise old businessman thought for a second and said, "Certainly, my son, one word—'experience.' "

The young man said, "Please, sir, permit me one more question. How do you get experience?"

The wise old businessman said, "Son, two words—'bad decisions.' "

Money is spiritual. Money is worldly. How we handle our finances will greatly influence the fulfillment we find in life. I keep this piece entitled "Money and You" close to our family's heart:

Money can buy medicine, but not health.
Money can buy a house, but not a home.
Money can buy companionship, but not a friend.
Money can buy entertainment, but not happiness.
Money can buy food, but not an appetite.
Money can buy a bed, but not sleep.
Money can buy a crucifix, but not a savior.
Money can buy the good life, but not eternal life.[6]

DISCUSSION STARTERS

1. When you were growing up, did your family have any kind of stewardship plan?

_____

_____

_____

_____

_____

2. What have you done to teach the concept of stewardship to
   your children?

   _____

   _____

   _____

   _____

   _____

3. Which section of this chapter challenged you the most?

   _____

   _____

   _____

   _____

   _____

4. What decisions do you need to make as a family about your
   finances?

   _____

   _____

   _____

   _____

   _____

5. What is the significance of the following Scripture? How can
   these words of Jesus help your family with your finances?

   For where your treasure is, there your heart will be also.
   No one can serve two masters. . . . Either he will hate the
   one and love the other, or he will be devoted to the one
   and despise the other. You cannot serve both God and
   Money (Matt. 6:21,24).

   _____

   _____

   _____

   _____

   _____

10

Energize Your Family's Spiritual Growth

We were the only family with children in the restaurant. I sat Erik in a high chair. Suddenly Erik squealed and said, "Hi there." He pounded his hands on the high-chair tray and wriggled and giggled with merriment. I looked around and saw the source of his merriment. It was a man with a tattered rag of a coat—dirty, greasy and worn. His pants were baggy with a zipper at half-mast, and his toes poked out of would-be shoes. His shirt was dirty and his hair uncombed and unwashed. His whiskers were too short to be called a beard and his nose was so varicose, it looked like a roadmap. We were too far from him to smell him, but I was sure he smelled. His hands waved and flapped on loose wrists.

"Hi there, baby. I see ya, buster," the man said to Erik. My husband and I exchanged looks that said, "What do we do?" Everyone in the restaurant noticed and looked at us and then at the man. The old geezer was creating a nuisance with my beautiful baby. Our meal came, and the man began shouting across the room, "Do ya know patty-cake? Do ya know peekaboo? Hey, look, he knows peekaboo."

Nobody thought the old man was cute. He was obviously drunk. My husband and I were embarrassed. We ate in silence, all except for Erik, who was running through his repertoire for the admiring skid-row bum, who in turn reciprocated with his cute comments.

We finally got through the meal and headed for the door. My husband went to pay the check and told me to meet him in the parking lot. The old man sat poised between me and the door. "Lord, just let me out of here before he speaks to me or Erik," I prayed. As I drew closer to the man, I turned my back trying to sidestep him and avoid any air he might be breathing. As I did, Erik leaned over my arm, reaching with both arms in a baby's pick-me-up position. Before I could stop him, Erik had propelled himself from my arms into the man's.

Suddenly a very smelly old man and a very young baby consummated their love relationship. Erik, in an act of total trust, love and submission, laid his tiny head upon the man's ragged shoulder. The man's eyes closed, and I saw tears hover beneath his lashes. His aged hands, full of grime, pain and hard labor, gently, so gently, cradled my baby's bottom and stroked his back. No two beings have ever loved so deeply for so short a time. I stood awestruck. The old man rocked and cradled Erik in his arms for a moment, and then his eyes opened and set squarely on mine. He said in a firm commanding voice, "You take care of this baby."

Somehow I managed to say, "I will," from a throat that contained a stone. He pried Erik from his chest unwillingly, longingly, as though he were in pain. I received my baby, and the man said, "God bless you, ma'am, you've just given me my Christmas gift." I said nothing more than a muttered thanks.

With Erik in my arms, I ran for the car. My husband was wondering why I was crying and holding Erik so tightly, and why I was saying, "My God, my God, forgive me." I had just witnessed Christ's love shown through the innocence of a tiny child who saw no sin, who made no judgment, a child who saw a soul and a mother who saw a suit of clothes. I was a Christian who was blind, holding a child who was not. I felt it was God asking, "Are you willing to share your son for a moment?" when He shared His for eternity. The ragged old man, unwittingly, had reminded me that to enter the kingdom of God, we must become as little children.

—Author unknown

● ● ●

We can learn so much about our own spirituality from our children. Their faith is fresh and beautiful. Yet even though the faith of a child is refreshing, it is so easy for parents to be distracted when it comes to helping our kids grow spiritually.

A woman met with me to talk about her daughter, who was struggling with an eating disorder called anorexia. Basically, the young girl was starving herself to death. During our conversation, the mother mentioned that she herself had had more than $18,000 worth of cosmetic surgery during the past year. She said she decided to get everything taken care of at once. She was proud of her new pair of eyes, smaller nose, fuller lips and larger bra size! When I suggested that her daughter was in dire need of counseling, the mother told me she couldn't afford counseling for her daughter. Wouldn't you agree with me that her priorities were just a bit off?

It is clear in the Bible that the primary role of a parent is to train children who will not only be faithful to their relationship with God but who will also develop their own vital, vibrant faith.

One of my greatest fears is that families aren't investing the time and energy it takes to leave a spiritual legacy for their children. The average family simply does not take a proactive role in building up the spiritual lives of their children. We may spend thousands of dollars and hundreds of hours on important issues like vacations, business plans and home improvement; but when it comes to spiritual values, we too often allow circumstances and chance to affect how we manage our family life and especially how we handle the spiritual side of our family legacy.

"Unless the LORD builds the house, its builders labor in vain" (Ps. 127:1). That's one of the greatest pieces of advice from the psalms of the Old Testament. It is very clear in the Bible that the primary role of a parent is to train children who will not only be faithful to their relationship with God but who will also develop their own vital, vibrant faith. Far too many parents expect the church to instill the spiritual values their children need. In a national study done by FamilyLife, Christian families expressed that their number one need was assistance in helping their children grow spiritually.[1] Most parents have a difficult time proactively helping their children grow spiritually because they themselves didn't have adequate role models growing up.

Set the Pace of Spiritual Leadership in Your Home

Usually, your children's faith is very dependent on the examples they see at home. In other words, *you* set the pace of spiritual leadership in your home. If you desire your children to have vibrant spiritual lives, then they need to see an authentic faith lived out in their family. No one expects you to be perfect, but you shouldn't expect them to follow a hypocrite either. Consider the following questions. They will help you evaluate your own spiritual disciplines.

How Is Your Time with God?

How long has it been since you gave God a portion of undisturbed, uninterrupted time and listened to His voice? We have a photograph of our daughter Heidi sitting on the living room sofa holding the Bible upside down, pretending she was reading it. She could barely walk and definitely couldn't read. When Cathy and I asked her what she was reading, she said, "I'm doing my 'votions." This is the same chair Cathy used when she did her devotions. Children see; children do.

Apparently, Jesus made time with the Father an absolute priority. He spent regular time praying and listening. Mark reveals, "Very early in the morning, while it was still dark, Jesus got up, left the house and went off to a solitary place, where he prayed" (Mark 1:35). Luke tells us, "Jesus often withdrew to lonely places and prayed" (Luke 5:16). Let me ask the obvious: If Jesus, the Son of God, thought it worthwhile to clear His calendar to pray, wouldn't we be wise to do the same?

I asked one of the busiest women I know how she manages to get so much done in the day. She smiled and showed me her schedule. It read, "6:00 A.M.-6:45 A.M. Quiet Time." She had let me in on a secret. Her strength and her stamina came from her time alone with God each morning.

One of my hobbies is reading biographies of great women and men of the Christian faith. They come in all shapes, sizes, denominations and styles; but the one thing they all have in common is a regular, daily time with God.

Do You Have a Supportive, Spiritual Accountability Relationship?
Life is difficult, and living out a vibrant, contagious faith is not
easy. I find that parents who do a good job of building a spiritual
legacy often have a support and accountability system to help
them be more effective as the spiritual leaders of the family.

I am currently involved in a weekly support and accountability group with three other men. When we first started the group,
we talked about politics and sports and only briefly mentioned
our faith and family issues. One day, one of the group members
opened up to tell us he was struggling with his marriage; and from
that day on, it has been a much more focused, supportive and
deeper-sharing group. I will never forget the day I shared that I felt
Cathy's and my marriage was a bit stagnant. When I left the meeting, one of the men called me on my cell phone and said, "You and
Cathy need to get away and get some time together. If it's finances
or babysitting, we'll take care of it. When can you go?" That's the
kind of support we all need, even if it's humbling.

Some support and accountability relationships use questions
like the ones below to make sure they're staying on the right track:

- Have you been with a woman/man anywhere this past
  week that might appear compromising?
- Have any of your financial dealings lacked integrity?
- Have you exposed yourself to any sexually explicit material?
- Have you spent adequate time in Bible study and prayer?
- Have you given priority time to your family?
- Have you fulfilled the mandates of your calling?
- Have you just lied to me?

Do You Have a Person with Whom You Pray on a Regular Basis?
We have found that our involvement with a couples' group from
our church has been a wonderful source of friendship, support
and sharing of parenting ideas. Our group is made up of five couples who all have children about the same age. We've studied parenting and marriage resources together, as well as other Bible
study materials. It is always amazing how often our parenting,

marriage and spiritual-life issues come up no matter what material we are using. These couples are helping us be better parents to our children, and they're challenging us to build a spiritual legacy.

I remember a season in my life when I was extremely busy and had little accountability. Cathy challenged me by reminding me I had lots of acquaintances and very few friends. She suggested that I get together with a man at my work named John. I told her John was way too busy to spend any kind of regular time with me, but she kept pressing me to speak with him. We ended up meeting for lunch every Wednesday for over three years until he moved away. Our Wednesday lunch was never structured. We talked, shared our week's experiences, perhaps discussed a problem or two and then prayed together. I loved those times, and they made me a better husband, father and focused Christian. Today, John and I see each other every two months because of distance, and we keep the relationship close through phone calls and periodic visits. Over the years, those times together have become very meaningful.

Do You and Your Spouse Have a Regular Time with God Together? Most couples I know struggle to spend quality spiritual time together. It is easy to get so distracted with the pace of life that we miss building a spiritual relationship with our spouse. Cathy and I have tried almost every kind of devotional time together, but most of our experiments have fizzled. However, we've come across a method that may not sound spiritual enough for some, but it works for us.

It is easy to get so distracted with the pace of life that we miss building a spiritual relationship with our spouse.

First of all, we try to pray together daily for our kids and for ourselves. Prayer connects us with God and with each other, and it focuses us on the right priority of developing the spirituality of our children. Second, each week we go through a meeting plan that is very conversational and relational—and separate from our Bible study and individual quiet times with God. We work through the list below, and we do not need to prepare ahead of time. We'd rather have our time together in a peaceful setting, but we've been known to hold this weekly meeting while driving, watching one of the children's games or even—when I am traveling—on the phone. We both look forward to our weekly spiritual and relational connection. Use this list as a jumping-off point for your time with your spouse; every couple needs to find what works best for them. You can also check out our book *Closer* for more in-depth ideas on how to spiritually connect with each other.

Jim and Cathy—Weekly Meeting

- Devotional times for the week
- Greatest joy of the week
- Greatest struggle of the week
- An affirmation
- A wish or a hope
- Physical goals
- Prayer

Devotional times for the week. This is a chance for us to share with each other what we've been learning. Cathy often wants to contribute something from her Bible study that she thinks will be meaningful to me. These moments are often very encouraging and give us a chance to report what spiritual input has come into our lives during the week. Because of this time of sharing, we're often looking for something during our personal times with God to bring to each other, and it keeps us much more in tune with where we are in our individual journeys with Him.

Greatest joy of the week. Usually, Cathy's greatest joy is centered on the kids. Most of the time, my joy is also kid-related. It gives us a chance each week to be reminded of the many blessings we have in our family, ministry, friendships and the events of our life.

Greatest struggle of the week. This can be anything from an irritation to a deep longing, from an in-depth family problem to a personal struggle. There have been times when Cathy has said, "My greatest struggle of the week is you." That's when we need to move out of the devotional time and have one of those conversations to deal with whatever issue needs to be discussed; then we come back to the devotional time. I actually look forward to sharing a struggle. It's a great time of support and strength as I share on a deeper level with my wife.

An affirmation. We try to take a few moments to affirm one another each week. One of my primary love languages is words of affirmation (see the discussion on the five love languages in chapter 6). I know that even with our busy lifestyle, at least once a week Cathy will focus on giving me a word of encouragement. Our weekly meeting is a great time to reflect on the reasons we married and on our partnership with God in parenting our children, and to meet each other's needs with words of love and encouragement.

A wish or a hope. This can go pretty much in any direction. It can be very deep regarding our relationship with a family member or something as simple as the colors we would like for the new car. I've found that this portion of our weekly meeting can be lighter than the struggle of the week, but often it goes in the same direction.

Physical goals. Both Cathy and I are conscious of the fact that our bodies are the "temple of the Holy Spirit" (1 Cor. 6:19), so we're constantly trying to work on these temples. We take a few moments to share our physical goals with each other and either cheer each other on or help each other be accountable to our established goals. During the writing of this book, Cathy has needed to keep me accountable more than she has needed to cheer me on, since some of the physical disciplines have been lacking in my life.

Prayer. After sharing these different areas of our life with each other and with God, now we're ready to pray. We try to focus on adoration and thanksgiving as well as supplication and requests. Prayer brings couples and families together, and prayer focuses us on our real priorities instead of the false priorities that so often get in the way of seeing what's truly important in our lives.

Focus on the Spiritual Life of Your Family

Why are most families more proactive with sports and school than we are with the spiritual development of our children? Because focusing on the spiritual life of our families doesn't come naturally for many, even for those who desperately want that focus. Over the years, I've asked hundreds of people how or if their families of origin had any kind of spiritual life together—I asked more out of desperation for my own family than because of a need to gather information for some type of study. By far, the most common answer was "We prayed before meals, my parents took us to church and that was about it."

Neither Cathy nor I grew up in families that were active in church. We didn't have role models in this area of our lives, but we've found that even our friends who grew up in pastors' homes didn't experience much of a proactive approach to passing the spiritual torch to the next generation. Some had memories of a rigid devotional time that usually involved their father reading from the Bible or a devotional book. But when we've asked our friends about how they have energized their family's faith, most have just looked blank and haven't had a clue.

Developing children's spiritual lives was a vital part of ancient Hebrew culture. To this day, the most often quoted Scripture in an Orthodox Jewish home is the *Shema,* their confession of faith found in Deuteronomy 6:4-9; 11:13-21; and Numbers 15:37-41. Orthodox Jews quote parts or all of these passages every morning and evening. The *Shema* really is the very core of spiritual values for both the Jewish and Christian traditions. Deuteronomy 6:4-9 provides some important instructions for passing on our faith to our children:

> Hear, O Israel: The LORD our God, the LORD is one. Love the LORD your God with all your heart and with all your soul and with all your strength. These commandments that I give you today are to be upon your hearts. *Impress them on your children.* Talk about them when you sit at

home and when you walk along the road, when you lie down and when you get up. Tie them as symbols on your hands and bind them on your foreheads. Write them on the doorframes of your houses and on your gates (emphasis added).

We are to impress God's Word on our children's hearts, but how do we do that?

Today there is a fresh wind inspiring us to pass on our faith to our children in a positive way. Organizations such as HomeWord and Focus on the Family are coming alongside parents to help us light the fire of spiritual growth in our families.[2] In addition to recommending the help available from such organizations, I'd like to offer three suggestions that, if implemented, should significantly help promote the spiritual life of our families:

1. Develop a regular family devotional time
2. Develop a family constitution
3. Include God's presence in family renewal

Regular Family Devotional Time

As our babies moved toward childhood, Cathy and I tried to start having regular family devotional times. Usually it consisted of my reading the Bible or a story, and our kids were usually bored and voiced disapproval. Cathy and I would energetically try for a while, and then we would give up for long periods of time. We kept asking others what devotions they were doing as a family, but everyone we spoke to simply asked us to give them ideas if we ever came across something that worked.

One of the days that we managed to corral the girls, I read a brief Scripture and then a story from one of the devotional books that I'd written for teenagers. It bombed: In the middle of my story, the girls got in an argument, and Heidi fell asleep. I quit the story in the middle and gave up again!

That night, Cathy had an idea. She said, "Jim, with no offense to your devotionals—they are great for teens—the stuff you read isn't age-appropriate or interactive enough for our girls. I don't blame them for being bored." Ouch!

"What would you do?" I responded.

"Well, I think they have to participate, and we must make the devotional times more experiential. Our kids love Sunday School, and that's what they do in their classes."

"Okay, fine. How would you do it?"

"Let's have them act out a Bible story. No one ever said devotions have to be serious, and they definitely don't need a three-point sermon." Ouch, again! (It was only two points and a poem.)

So that night we pulled the kids back into Christy's bedroom for what seemed like Round 100 of Burns Family Devotions. Cathy said, "Tonight we are going to try something different for our family time. I want you to pick out a story and then rehearse it and act it out."

The girls' eyes lit up—everyone in our family is a frustrated movie star. Christy opened up her Bible storybook, and the first story was about Adam and Eve. "Let's do this one. I want to be Eve." Then the other girls chimed in that they also wanted to be Eve. No one wanted to be Adam; after all, he was a boy. Well, this started an argument among them.

I looked at Cathy and almost smiled that her idea wasn't working either. Then I said to Christy, "You are the oldest. Adam was older than Eve, so you are Adam." She asked if she could draw a mustache on her face, and I said sure. Rebecca and Heidi still both wanted to be Eve. I know that some of the Bible scholars reading this book won't like my answer, but I was desperate so I said, "Fine, Rebecca you will be Eve, and Heidi you will be Evette, Eve's little sister." They chose me to be the snake.

The girls went into our bedroom to rehearse, but all I could hear was arguing over what outfits they were going to wear. I still didn't have high hopes for family devotions Cathy-style. Finally, after some prodding, they paraded back into the main stage of Christy's room. Christy came in wearing one of my Hawaiian shirts, a baseball cap and a mustache painted in permanent marker (but that's another story!). Heidi strutted in wearing a Hawaiian hula outfit with the coconut shells for her top so crooked that they weren't covering what they were supposed to cover. The girls had definitely chosen a Hawaiian Garden of Eden theme.

Then six-year-old Rebecca made her appearance as Eve. She was wearing, well, uh, nothing. Rebecca was absolutely stark naked. She looked at us, put her hands on her hips and blurted out, "She wasn't wearing anything in the Garden, was she?" I looked at Cathy, and she looked at me. I said, "No, she wasn't; but, Rebecca, if you are ever asked to do this play in Sunday School, you can't wear your birthday suit."

Now that the actresses were in costume, we were ready to begin the play. As you can imagine, the play was a success—and that's pretty much how our children learned Bible stories. There were no more boring messages from Dad, and every devotional became interactive and experiential.

Now that our children are teenagers, we don't do plays, but our family devotionals are still very interactive. Sometimes we let our kids pick what we are going to do, because kids support what they help create. We also buy into the philosophy that kids learn best when *they* talk, not when *you* talk. What Cathy taught me that day—which has made all the difference for Burns family times—is to use whatever method your kids will enjoy and is age-appropriate. Lectures and sermons are out; interaction and discussions are in.

If you are having trouble with your family devotional time, then make an appointment with the youth worker or children's director at your church and ask for their favorite curriculum ideas or stories that would be age-appropriate for your kids. Make your time fun and spiritual.

As you pray together as a family and enjoy each other's company, you will pass on the heritage of faith to your children. The main thing is to have a regular family time together to focus on your faith and to follow the biblical mandate in Deuteronomy 6:7 to impress the Word of God on the next generation. (See the end of the chapter for five family devotions to get you started with your own family.)

A Family Constitution

The Constitution of the United States of America documents the foundational laws for governing our country. These are the basic, or essential, rules from which our government derives other laws. If a constitution is important for a country or a value statement is important for a business, then why don't more people create a family constitution? A family constitution is a written list of the important things you and your loved ones want out of your everyday relationships. When you think of your family's values and desires, what words describe what you would like your family to stand for?

If a constitution is important for a country or a value statement is important for a business, then why don't more people create a family constitution?

On one of our Burns family camping trips, we all took out sheets of paper and began to brainstorm what our Burns Family Constitution would look like. Just the activity of sharing ideas was very helpful and, frankly, quite insightful. We then came up with our own family constitution. We have it posted on our refrigerator. Periodically we need to be reminded of the commitment we made to each other to live by our constitution. No matter what the age of your children, let them take an active part in creating your own family constitution.

Burns Family Constitution
- Honor
- Trust
- Truthfulness and integrity
- Fruit of the Spirit:
  Love, joy, peace, patience, kindness, goodness, faithfulness, gentleness and self-control
- Support and encouragement
- Time together

- Sharing and generosity
- Respect
- Follow our moral code

God's Presence in Family Renewal

Parents who actively include God's presence in family renewal times tend to create families that are spiritually healthier than others. In his excellent book *The Seven Habits of Highly Effective Families,* Stephen Covey emphasizes the importance of family renewal, which he calls "family times" and "one-on-ones." Family renewal involves a look at the total wellbeing of a family. Parents can bring the Lord into the daily rituals of life such as going to bed, eating meals, driving and even doing chores. Parents who include God in their vacations, camps and retreats, books, family nights and even service to others create families whose children tend to have many happy memories of growing spiritually together. Children tend to feel more secure in their faith when God is a part of their everyday activities.[3]

As you look at Covey's diagram on the following page,[4] consider how your family is doing in each of the areas. What steps can you take to improve your family renewal? Lighting the fires of spiritual growth and wholeness in our children is a daily decision. It takes a great deal of work and energy to pass the torch of our faith to our children. Please be assured that it is never too late and definitely never too early to ignite the faith fires in the lives of our families. Often there is much we can learn from our kids. They are not looking for a perfect spiritual leader with absolute biblical knowledge, but they do want one who can help show them the way.

As my mother lay in her hospital bed preparing to die of the cancer that had taken over her body, I struggled with the thought of leaving her for one day to speak to 6,000 high school students in Colorado. I wanted to be near her when she died. As the speaking engagement drew closer, I was leaning toward not going because Mom was so sick. I even asked a friend to fill in for me if I couldn't attend. (The organizers of the conference where I was speaking were kind enough to allow a last-minute replacement if I chose to stay with Mom.)

Exercise together.
Do physical activities
together.
Reclarify expectations
and goals around
financial and physical
assets.

Love and affirm
one another.
Laugh at "inside jokes"
and relax together.
Build relationships
of trust and uncondi-
tional love.

Renew commitments.
Clarify directions
and goals.
Pray and worship
together.
Read inspirational or
sacred literature together.

Learn new things
together.
Share and discuss
ideas.

The day before I was scheduled to fly out, my mother took a
turn for the better. I had not seen her so alert for several weeks.
We talked about my trip, and she urged me, "Go and help all those
kids." She said, "I'll be fine and be right here when you get back."
I was torn; but I decided, with the prodding of my mom and dad,
that I should go and speak and return as soon as possible.

I stopped by my parents' home on the way to the airport. Mom
was sitting up in her hospital bed. We talked for a short time, and
then I turned to leave. She called me back to her bedside and in a
weak voice simply said, "Jimmy, I love you, and I'm very, very proud
of you."

That night after I spoke to the students, I walked back to my
hotel room where I got a call from Cathy telling me that my
mother had died. I made arrangements to fly back to California
earlier than planned and then tried to sleep.

Sometime in the middle of the night, I remembered her last words to me. What a blessing. What a spiritual giant.

You and I are to pass on the faith to the next generation. It's our highest calling and our God-given mandate.

DISCUSSION STARTERS

1. Describe the spiritual atmosphere of the home in which you grew up.

_____

_____

_____

_____

_____

_____

2. What areas of your own spiritual life could use some help?

_____

_____

_____

_____

_____

_____

_____

3. Have you tried family devotional times? If so, how did they work?

_____

_____

_____

_____

_____

_____

4. As you read the following biblical mandate to pass on the faith to your children, what specifically comes to your mind as action steps for your family?

Hear, O Israel: The LORD our God, the LORD is one. Love the LORD your God with all your heart and with all your soul and with all your strength. These commandments that I give you today are to be upon your hearts. Impress them on your children. Talk about them when you sit at home and when you walk along the road, when you lie down and when you get up. Tie them as symbols on your hands and bind them on your foreheads. Write them on the doorframes of your houses and on your gates (Deut. 6:4-9).

_____

_____

_____

_____

_____

_____

_____

Five Family Devotions

Are you ready to pass on the heritage of faith to your children? As you have a regular family devotional time, focus on your faith and teach your children God's Word. I have included five family devotions to help you get started.

1. Affirmation Bombardment

And let us consider how we may spur one another on toward love and good deeds. Let us not give up meeting together, as some are in the habit of doing, but let us encourage one another—and all the more as you see the Day approaching (Heb. 10:24-25).

Give words of affirmation and encouragement to each family member one at a time. Some families like to write out three positive, encouraging words about each person, share them verbally and then give the person what has been written.

2. Thank Therapy

Give thanks in all circumstances, for this is God's will for you in Christ Jesus (1 Thess. 5:18).

Have each family member write out 10 reasons that he or she is thankful and then share these reasons with the other family members.

3. Confession of Sin

If we confess our sins, he is faithful and just and will forgive us our sins and purify us from all unrighteousness (1 John 1:9).

According to this Scripture, as we confess our sins, God forgives us and absolutely cleanses us from those sins. Take a moment to have each family member privately write out on a piece of paper any of his or her sins that come to mind. Make sharing these sins optional. Have everyone fold up his or her paper and place it in a fire-resistant container. Then burn the papers to signify that God forgives our sins and wipes our slates clean.

Ask each family member to pray a prayer of thanksgiving for the forgiveness of sin.

4. Rock of Remembrance

Read the following Scriptures. What do they say about God? How do they apply to your life?

He is the Rock, his works are perfect, and all his ways are just. A faithful God who does no wrong, upright and just is he (Deut. 32:4).

The LORD is my rock, my fortress and my deliverer; my God is my rock, in whom I take refuge. He is my shield and the horn of my salvation, my stronghold (Ps. 18:2).

Many references in the Old Testament show that when the people of Israel had an encounter with God, they would build an altar made from rocks to remember God's presence. Ask each family member to find a rock and use it as a symbol of a significant commitment that he or she will make to God. Some people use their rock as a way of giving over to the Lord a specific fear or sin. Pile the rocks in a visible place as a way of remembering this special commitment and time with God.

5. The Encouragement Project

A new command I give you: Love one another. As I have loved you, so you must love one another (John 13:34).

As a family, choose someone who needs a little encouragement and come up with an idea to bring joy to that person's life. Our family decided to write notes of encouragement to a woman who had lost her husband a year earlier.

Endnotes

Chapter 1: The Power of Being There

1. According to a 2009 study done by the National Center on Addiction and Substance Abuse at Columbia University (CASA), teens who eat dinner with their families infrequently (fewer than three times per week) are twice as likely to use tobacco or marijuana and more than one and a half times likelier to have used alcohol than teens who have frequent family dinners (five to seven family dinners per week).
2. Max Lucado, *When Christ Comes* (Nashville, TN: Word Publishing, 1999), pp. 21-22.

Chapter 2: Parenting with Affection, Warmth and Encouragement

1. Ross Campbell, M.D., *How to Really Love Your Child* (Wheaton, IL: Victor Books, 1985), p. 73.
2. Thayer and Smith, "The KJV New Testament Greek Lexicon," *crosswalk.com,* 1995-2003. http://www.biblestudytools.net/Lexicons/Greek/grk.cgi?number=3870&version=kjv (accessed July 31, 2003).

Chapter 3: Build Healthy Morals and Values

1. "Alcohol and Other Drug Use Among High School Students," *The Journal of the American Medical Association* (December 18, 1991), p. 3266.
2. V. C. Strasburger, "Sex, Drugs, Rock 'n' Roll and the Media: Are the Media Responsible for Adolescent Behavior?" *Adolescent Medicine*, vol. 8 (1997), pp. 403-414.
3. Jeannie Echenique, "Early Dating May Lead to Early Sex," *USA Today*, November 12, 1986, p. D1.
4. Candyce Stapen, "Speaking Frankly Isn't Being Permissive," *USA Today*, November 3, 1986, p. D6.
5. Rob Stein, "Abstinence-only Programs Might Work, Study Says," *The Washington Post,* February 2, 2010. http://www.washingtonpost.com/wp-dyn/content/article/2010/02/01/AR2010020102628.html.
6. "Generation M^2: Media in the Lives of 8- to 18-Year Olds," Kaiser Family Foundation, January 2010. http://www.kff.org/entmedia/upload/8010.pdf.
7. Jim Burns, *Uncommon Youth Ministry* (Ventura: Regal Publishing, 2001), p. 216.
8. "The Stats on Internet Pornography," Online Schools. http://www.onlinemba.com/blog/stats-on-internet-pornography/.
9. For a more comprehensive look at creating a media-safe home, get the free download of "Creating a Media Safe Home" from my book *Teenology: The Art of Raising Great Teenagers* at www.homeword.com.
10. Stephen Arterburn and Jim Burns, *How to Talk to Your Kids About Drugs* (Eugene, OR: Harvest House Publishers, 2007), p. 24.
11. "Teens Who Smoke Seem Likely to Take Other Risks," *The Orange County (California) Register*, April 25, 1995, Health and Science section.

Chapter 4: Discipline with Consistency

1. Lee Pitts, "These Things I Wish," from Jack Canfield, et al., *Chicken Soup for the Golden Soul: Heartwarming Stories for People 60 and Over* (Deerfield Beach, FL: HCI, 2000).
2. James Dobson, *Family News from Dr. James Dobson* (February 1994), p. 1.

Chapter 5: Ruthlessly Eliminate Stress

1. Richard A. Swenson, *Margin: Restoring Emotional, Physical, Financial, and Time Reserves to Overloaded Lives* (Colorado Springs, CO: NavPress, 1995), p. 13.

2. This essay has been attributed to Brother Jeremiah, a friar at Graymoor Monastery, among other people. This version was quoted in Ted W. Engstrom, *The Pursuit of Excellence* (Grand Rapids, MI: Zondervan Publishing House, 1982), p. 90.

3. Archibald Hart, *Stress and Your Child* (Nashville, TN: Word Publishing, 1992), p. 8.

4. Ibid., pp. 18-19. Reprinted by permission of the publisher.

Chapter 6: Communication Is the Key

1. Gary Chapman, *The Five Love Languages: How to Express Heartfelt Commitment to Your Mate* (Chicago: Northfield Publishing, 1992), pp. 202-203.

2. Ibid.

3. Dolores Curran, *Traits of a Healthy Family* (New York: Ballantine Books, 1984).

Chapter 7: Play Is Necessary for a Close-Knit Family

1. Mike Yaconelli, *Dangerous Wonder* (Colorado Spring, CO: NavPress, 2003).

2. Leonard Sweet, *Learn to Dance the Soul Salsa* (Grand Rapids, MI: Zondervan Publishing House, 2000), p. 158.

Chapter 8: Love Your Spouse

1. Leonard Sweet, *Learn to Dance the Soul Salsa* (Grand Rapids, MI: Zondervan Publishing House, 2000).

2. Les Parrott, *Saving Your Marriage Before It Starts* (Grand Rapids, MI: Zondervan Publishing, 1995), n.p.; also found in Les Parrott, "Why the Soul of a Good Marriage So Often Aches" in *When Bad Things Happen to Good Marriages* (Grand Rapids, MI: Zondervan Publishing, 2001), n.p.

3. Willard F. Harley, Jr., *His Needs, Her Needs* (Grand Rapids, MI: Fleming H. Revell Company, 1988).

4. Billy Graham, spoken at a crusade that was aired on television.

Chapter 9: The Best Things in Life Are Not Things

1. Howard Dayton, *Your Money Counts* (Longwood, FL: Crown Ministries, 1996), p. 34.

2. Ron and Judy Blue, *Money Matters for Parents and Their Kids* (Nashville, TN: Thomas Nelson, 1988), p. 47.

3. Ibid, p. 45.

4. U.S. Department of the Treasury, "The Debt to the Penny and Who Holds It," *Bureau of the Public Debt Online*, June 30, 2003. http://www.publicdebt.treas.gov/opd/opd pdodt.htm (accessed July 1, 2003).

5. Dayton, *Your Money Counts*, p. 129. Reprinted by permission of the publisher, Crown Financial Ministries.

6. Author unknown.

Chapter 10: Energize Your Family's Spiritual Growth

1. "Family Needs Survey," 2002, as reported by the Church and Community department of FamilyLife.

2. For more information, see the HomeLight resources by Jim Burns (Ventura, CA: Gospel Light Publishers, 2010).

3. Stephen R. Covey, *The Seven Habits of Highly Effective Families* (New York: Golden Books, 1997), pp. 279-280.

4. Ibid., p. 281. Reprinted by permission of the publisher.

Devotionals from Jim Burns

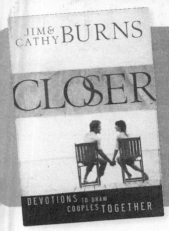

Closer: Devotions to Draw Couples Together

Closer is the new approach to couple's devotionals. 52 devotions cover real marriage topics - such as healthy conflict, spiritual connection, and sexual fulfillment - and are designed to fit into most any schedule. Full of scripture verses, engaging stories and practical action steps, each entry will inspire faith conversations: those quiet talks so vital for emotional and spiritual intimacy in marriage.

One Life

Your kids only have one life – help them discover the greatest adventure life has to offer! 50 fresh devotional readings that cover many of the major issues of life and faith your kids are wrestling with such as sex, family relationships, trusting God, worry, fatigue and daily surrender. And it's perfect for you and your kids to do together!

Addicted to God

Is your kids' time absorbed by technology, text messaging and hanging out at the mall? This devotional will challenge them to adopt thankfulness, make the most of their days and never settle for mediocrity! Fifty days in the Scripture is bound to change your kids' lives forever.

Devotions on the Run

These devotionals are short, simple, and spiritual. They will encourage you to take action in your walk with God. Each study stays in your heart throughout the day, providing direction and clarity when it is most needed.

90 Days Through the New Testament ebook

Downloadable devotional. Author Jim Burns put together a Bible study devotional program for himself to follow, one that would take him through the New Testament in three months. His simple plan was so powerful that he was called to share it with others. A top seller!

Tons of helpful resources for parents and youth.
Visit our online store at www.HomeWord.com
Or call us at 800-397-9725

HOME WORD
WHERE PARENTS GET REAL ANSWERS

Small Group Curriculum Kits

Confident Parenting Kit

help you to tackle overcrowded lives, negative family patterns, while creating a grace-filled home and raising kids who love God and themselves.

Kit contains:

guide and participant guides

Creating an Intimate Marriage Kit

Dr. Jim Burns wants every couple to experience a marriage filled with A.W.E.: affection, warmth, and encouragement. He shows husbands and wives how to make their marriage a priority as they discover ways to repair the past, communicate and resolve conflict, refresh their marriage spiritually, and more!

Kit contains:

guide and participant guides

Parenting Teenagers for Positive Results

This popular resource is designed for small groups and Sunday

humorous family vignettes followed by words of wisdom by youth and family expert, Jim Burns, Ph.D.

Kit contains:

guide and participant guides

10 Building Blocks Kit

the 10 essential principles for creating a solid, close-knit household,

Use this curriculum to help equip families in your church.

Kit contains:

guide and participant guides

Tons of helpful resources for youth workers, parents and youth. Visit our online store at www.HomeWord.com or call us at 800-397-9725 Call for bulk discounts.

Pure Foundations from Jim Burns and HomeWord

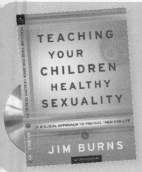

Teaching Your Children Healthy Sexuality Kit

Trusted family authority Dr. Jim Burns outlines a simple and practical guide for parents on how to develop in their children a healthy perspective regarding their bodies and sexuality. Promotes godly values about sex and relationships.

Kit contains:

guide and participant guides

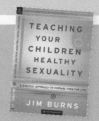

Teaching Your Children Healthy Sexuality book

sexual

extend

Parents will learn how to promote godly values about sex and

The Purity Code Book ...ages 10-14

Read *The Purity Code* together and discuss the questions at the

Accept Nothing Less ...ages 14+

Jim Burns encourages young readers not to settle for second emphasizing
and involves the heart and mind as well. Offering straight Accept

The Purity Code Audio

Jim Burns   FOUNDATIONS

goes beyond the printed word with this unique audio

sexuality.

experts

Dr. John Townsend, Shannon Ethridge, Rebecca St. James, Hayley DiMarco and Doug Fields.

er